Here Am I;
Send Me

A brief personal account of life
at Temple Israel for the past 25 years
with some writings that have accentuated
the issues, the concerns, the feelings, and the growth
that has been ours

by
Rabbi Max A. Shapiro

Temple Israel
Minneapolis, Minnesota

And I heard the voice of the Lord saying:
Whom shall I send,
And who will go for us?
Then I said: "Here am I; send me".

(Isaiah 6:8)

This publication has been made possible
by Rabbi Shapiro's Discretionary Fund.

To Bernice

without whom there would have been nothing, and nothing would have mattered.

Thank You

My thanks to all of you who at some time over the past years made a contribution to the Rabbi's Discretionary Fund and thereby made the publication of this book possible.

To my colleagues and associates at Temple who saw to it that the programs we initiated were brought into being.

To Charlotte Moses, my secretary, who typed and retyped and whose reactions and responses to what I had written were always valuable.

To Patty Moses, Charlotte's daughter, who took the typewritten page and by her creativity and skill in production made it into the attractive and readable book now in your hands.

To Bernice, who read the manuscript and for her sharp eye, her perceptiveness and sensitivity and her thoughtful criticisms.

To Steven, our son, who also read the manuscript and whose evaluation, suggestions and approval have always been important to me.

And to all of you in the congregation with whom I have shared so much.

Table Of Contents

Most of the photographs
found in this volume
by Ivan Kalman

INTRODUCTION
Winter, 1980

As many of you know, I was ordained at the Hebrew Union College — Jewish Institute of Religion in Cincinnati in June, 1955. I was then 38 years old, approximately ten to twelve years older than the other members of my class. Bernice and I had been married almost eleven years, and we had two children. Susan was eight; Steven was five. At that time, as far as I could tell, we were the oldest family to have made it through the five years of Reform Rabbinic training.

Some months prior, the "match-up" between congregations and senior rabbinic students began. Of all that were available there were three that seemed most promising to Bernice and me: Dr. Nelson Glueck, President of HUC-JIR had asked me to become Assistant to the President at our school in New York; Dr. Victor Reichert, the Rabbi at the prestigious Rockdale Avenue Temple in Cincinnati and Warren Heldman, its president, had asked me to be the Associate Rabbi at Rockdale where I had been Director of Religious Education during my last years at the College-Institute; and Temple Israel in Minneapolis was looking for an Assistant Rabbi.

I came to Minneapolis on December 19, 1954 to meet with a Selection Committee. We met at the "old" Sheiks Restaurant for dinner and the next afternoon for lunch with the entire Board of Trustees at the Dyckman Hotel. Then I had a brief talk with Rabbi Minda in his office, and I was on my way back to Cincinnati.

It did not take long for Bernice and me to decide what we should do. Though it was flattering to be asked by Rockdale Temple to be an Associate Rabbi immediately upon ordination, we were anxious to leave Cincinnati. The New York School was very attractive, but I had not become a rabbi to be an administrator. And we did not relish the idea of living in Manhattan or the commuting that New York suburban life required.

Minneapolis was something else. We knew absolutely nothing about it, for in 1954 it did not have the national reputation it now enjoys. We rushed to the Farmer's Almanac to check the temperatures and the weather. We realized it would be cold, but we could not imagine how cold that would be. We read about the lakes and the Indians, but could find little about the Jewish community. All we were sure of was that there were some 750-800 families in the congregation and that its reputation in the Reform movement could not be surpassed.

What swayed us most in making our choice were three considerations. I had reported to Bernice that everyone I had met in Minneapolis was not only friendly and hospitable, but was understanding, helpful and accepting as well; and that though it was only 20 degrees above zero on that December 19, "it was not really that cold." The greatest attraction, however, was the possibility — "if we like you and you like us", was the way the Committee put it — that we would remain at Temple Israel for the rest of our rabbinic career. And so a few days later, when Charlie Goldstein who was Temple president called me and offered me the position as Assistant Rabbi, we readily accepted. In May, 1955, Bernice and I came to Minneapolis to attend the Temple's annual meeting, to be introduced to the congregation, and to look for housing. On June 16, with our two children, we came to make it our home.

Although I had the opportunity to speak from time to time at our Summer Services in 1955 — if you recall they were held in the Deinard Chapel on Friday evenings from 8:00 to 8:30 p.m. — I did not give a formal sermon until Rosh Hashanah of that year. The year before I had spoken at Rockdale Temple on the Holy Days and my sermons, as far as I could tell, had been very well received. And so I thought that with just a bit of updating, I could easily use the same talks. After all, the theme and meaning of Rosh Hashanah and Yom Kippur had not changed, though my position had.

Though I was certain that I was well prepared for my "debut" at Temple, when Rosh Hashanah was two weeks away I began to hiccup. And I could not stop. All I could think of was the disaster of my first sermon. I went off to see Dr. Reuben Berman who sent me to Dr. Oscar Lipschultz for x-rays. I don't recall now what the results were, but the Holy Days passed with no incidents, except the realization that though a sermon may be eminently successful in one congregation in one part of the country, it is not assured similar success elsewhere. That was the first of much knowledge and wisdom I have acquired at Temple.

Over the past twenty-five years I have given hundreds of talks, and I have always spoken directly to the congregation with no thought of publication or use of the sermons for any other purpose. I have not written essays or lectures to be read from the pulpit, but rather what I hoped would be conversations between me and each one of you. I have tried to prepare meticulously — most often I was able to — and to select my subjects with care and variety. To do otherwise would have been an insult to you and demeaning to me. And Bernice, who was always a faithful listener, would have suffered more than either of us.

Often I have tried to put myself in your place and have asked myself "What is the pulpit for? What is it that I should be hearing were I in the congregation?" My answer has been my hope that, at times, you have been instructed, edified, enlightened, stimulated, discomforted, comforted, angered, sensitized, amazed, spiritualized, and uplifted. I hope you have been spurred to some kind of religious commitment by what I may have said and that somehow your lives and relationships have been bettered because of it.

In this little volume I have selected a few sermons that reflect some of my thoughts and concerns during the past twenty-five years. I have also included a number of "Rabbi's Messages" that have appeared in our Temple "News". They, too, show something of the variety of issues that have made these years interesting, exciting and meaningful for me.

Bernice and I send you this volume as we begin our twenty-sixth year with you. We send it with our love, and with gratefulness that you have given us the privilege of living among you, of serving you and being your friend.

God bless.

Sermons

*Following the High Holy Days of 1964 I sent the congregation the three
sermons I gave during that period, and I now include two of them in this
volume.*

*"Religion and Politics" which was published in the **American Jewish
World** and subsequently in a number of other Jewish publications was
provoked by the presidential campaign of that year. I was careful — as I
always am — about not endorsing a candidate, but there were moral
issues that needed exposure. If you recall, Barry Goldwater was the
Republican nominee, and he had the full support of the Birchites, the
segregationists and the "right wingers" who were then agitating to make
religious observances an integral part of our public school systems.*

*Though Mr. Goldwater was defeated, the issues did not go away.
They were an underlying theme of the election of 1980. Note also the
word "Negro." It went out of use in the early 1970's.*

*My father, of blessed memory, died in February, 1964. "Death
Teaches Life" was the talk I gave at Yizkor Services that Yom Kippur. I
reread it very often.*

* * * *

Religion and Politics
September 6, 1964

There are many thoughts in my mind as I stand in this place
tonight — many thoughts and many feelings. I look about me
and see a congregation that is both precious and beloved. I see
among you dear friends whose lives have become so much a part
of mine — friends with whom I have shared moments of joy and
moments of sorrow; moments of laughter and moments of
learning; moments of prayer, moments of love.

And I see among you also many whom I know well, but into
whose lives I have not yet intimately walked. I pray that the year
ahead will bring us closer. And then there are some of you whom
I do not know. Every now and again I thumb through our Temple
Directory, checking the names I do not recognize. And I say to
myself, "Why don't I know these folks? Have I been neglecting

3

them? Have they been neglecting me? Where can we make amends?" And I tuck your names away in my memory, hoping that we will get to know each other soon.

And, of course, there are among you new members of the Temple — there are guests and visitors. To you, may I say "Welcome." "Welcome to our Temple." "Welcome to our Service." "Welcome as we face together the New Year — these awesome moments of self-examination, of searching the future."

I Am a Partisan

I have tormented myself much these past days, even as I do every year at this time. For this is a great responsibility I have — to be privileged to lay before you my deepest feelings and concern, to share with you the insights to Judaism that are mine. And the responsibility I feel is especially great this Rosh Hashanah. We are in an election year. In just two months you and I will be deciding issues that will direct our country and affect our lives for four years, at least, and perhaps for as long as we live, and our children live and their children. This is an election year — and there are partisans among you, just as there should be. And I am a partisan, too. Would you want me to be less?

Yes, I am a partisan. But this evening, I am not a political partisan. This Rosh Hashanah eve I speak neither for the Democrats nor the Republicans. But I am a partisan. I am a partisan for what I believe religion to be — for religion in general, and Judaism in particular. I am a partisan for what Judaism demands and teaches. For these, I believe, are vital for the time in which we live.

We have been blessed with life, you and I. But that in itself is of no special merit. It is not our purpose just to live! Our lives need direction! You would be the first to admit the foolishness of wandering aimlessly about when seeking a destination. You would be the first to get a map. Isn't it just as foolish to live one's life without direction — without a map or a guide of some kind?

And Judaism is just that! It is a guide for living that has been charted carefully and thoughtfully over thousands of years. It is a good guide. True. Authentic. And that is what makes our faith so important — so necessary. That is what it means to be a Jew — to follow the direction that Judaism has plotted. That is why this Temple exists — to help give our lives that direction. For Judaism is not just a set of beliefs. It is not just a conglomeration of ceremonies or an array of ritual. Judaism speaks about life. It makes demands upon our lives. And I am a partisan — partisan to the demands that Judaism makes.

And so when I come to this pulpit to speak to you I do not speak out of a vacuum, without a central commitment, without a clearly defined framework. Often I speak about Judaism. Often I speak for Judaism. But primarily — most of all — I speak because of Judaism. I speak because I am compelled — because Judaism is never silent on the issues that affect our lives. For if a religion cannot be relevant, if it cannot speak meaningfully to us, if it cannot provide us with a proper perspective to living, then it is dead! If Judaism cannot do all this, we had better close up this Temple and go home! We are wasting our time!

"All right, rabbi," you say, "don't get so excited. We'll have it your way. Religion is relevant. Judaism is pertinent. It does speak about every aspect of our lives — but stay away from politics. That's dynamite. You can be a partisan about anything that you want — go ahead, get high blood pressure — but politics? Not that!"

Politics and Religion

When I speak to you about anti-Semitism, I am a partisan, am I not? And yet I am speaking about politics. For there are candidates for public office who are often openly, and too often clandestinely, anti-Semitic. There are candidates for public office who cravenly accept the support of the anti-Semites and thereby give them importance and reason for being. Do I keep quiet about this? Should I be silent then?

When I speak to you about groups who are Hitler's heirs, whose history and philosophy, whose growth and tactics are too frightfully reminiscent of Nazism, I am a partisan. And I am speaking about politics. For these groups seek power. And power is sealed in the ballot box. Should I keep quiet about this? Should I be silent then?

When I speak about Russian tyranny toward the Soviet Jew, when I speak of anti-Jewish measures in the Argentine, when I decry Nasser's oft-repeated pledge to destroy Israel and all its inhabitants, I am a partisan. But I speak of politics. Our country has a diplomatic relation with each one of these. But should I keep quiet about this? Should I be silent then?

And when I speak to you about human brutality that is legally condoned, when I speak about atomic bombing and fallout, when I plead for freedom of religion, I am a partisan. And I am talking about politics. For these are decisions made in politics. These are decisions which deeply affect our lives. And because they affect our lives, Judaism must speak out about them. You may disagree with what it says, but should I, who have the responsibility to speak because of Judaism, should I, who am compelled to speak, be silent? Should I be quiet about these? Should I divorce our religion from life even though some might prefer it that way?

"Let the rabbi read Services," they say. "Let him lead a class in Jewish history. That is religion. Let him bless a Bar Mitzvah boy or officiate at a funeral. Let him pray piously. Let him sing the 'Shema' with gusto. That is religion."

Is that what Judaism is to you? — the reading of Services, the story of the past, the ritual at ceremonies, the observance of Holy Days. These are part of Judaism — a deeply beloved part for me. But they are not the sum total. They are not even basic. Unless we show concern for human life, unless we show concern for the sanctity of life, we have no religion. All we have is a cult — and a backward look!

No religion can exist in silence side by side with exploitation, with tyranny, with bigotry and with poverty. No religion can exist in silence side by side with disdain for other men, disrespect for their humanity, dispassion for their needs. These are matters that concern us because they are religious — and we are Jews! These are matters that concern us because they are political — and we are voters! We cannot today completely separate one from the other. Politics deals with virtually every aspect of man. And so does religion!

Actually that is what religion is all about — man! Man as he relates to himself. Man as he relates to his fellow man. Man as he relates to God. And politics is today involved in these same relationships. Political platforms make promises about them. Political organizations formulate plans about them. Political candidates stake their careers on them. Politics and religion have become intertwined. Issues of conscience and morality dominate the campaign. To whom do you listen? To the voice of the politician? Or to the voice of religion?

Man's Relationship to Man

Let us examine this factor of man's relationship to himself.

How does man relate to himself? "We'll tell you," says the John Birch Society, which has now become a political force. "We'll tell you. You lie, that's what. You lie. And the bigger the lie the better!"

What should man do? "We'll tell you," they say. "Create distrust. Don't trust the clergy. Don't trust your schools. Don't trust the press. Trust only us!"

How should man feel? "That's easy," they say. "Be wary of the stranger. Keep a careful eye on your neighbor. Only what we do is right. Only what the Birch Society wants is good."

Don't these people know? Have they not heard? There is a religious standard by which man should live. It is written large on every religious heart. What doth the Lord require of man?, "to do justly, to love mercy, to walk humbly."

Don't these Birchites know? Is it possible that no one has told them? Don't they understand that what the prophets proclaimed years ago is still true today. "The work of righteousness shall be peace; the effect of righteousness, quietness and confidence forever."

The John Birch Society may not know this. The words of the prophets may be foreign to them. But not to us. The voices of Amos and Micah, of Malachi and Isaiah have thundered in our ears for centuries. "Seek good and not evil," they cried. "Why do we deal treacherously every man against his brother?" And the fact is that the tentacles of treachery, the half truth, the big lie — the methods of the John Birch Society have been used, over and over again throughout history, to kill the innocent. They have been used against us! We have seen presumably good men, sane men, thoughtful men taken in by them. We have witnessed the lie bury justice, conquer friendships, foster hatreds. We have seen it create vicious anti-Semitism.

There are those who do not understand this. But we do. We Jews have been too much a part of history not to suspect the John Birch Society. We have seen too much, not to recognize the harbingers of hate who have gathered around it. We have been victims too often not to question those whom it supports. We know — as no others — that a society born in falsehood, nurtured on vilification and weened on rigid self-righteousness is a society that, in the long run, must resort to cruelty — must suppress men's thoughts and freedom!

Man's Relationship to His Fellow Man

The second factor in religion is man's relation to his fellow man.

How does man relate to his fellow man? "We'll tell you," says the avowed segregationist. "Don't give him his God-given rights — if he is black. Don't give him his constitutional rights — if he is black. Don't acknowledge that he is human — if he is black!"

What should man do? "We'll tell you," says the latent segregationist. "Support Civil Rights nationally but don't be so forceful at home. Censure the South, but be careful who moves into your neighborhood. Buy yourself a Freedom button, sign yourself a little pledge, as long as nothing happens close by."

How should man feel? "We'll tell you," they say. "Minneapolis is not Rochester nor Harlem nor Philadelphia. There is no trouble here. Let things stay the way they are. Why give a Negro a job? He can't do the work anyway. Why find him a place? The other employees will resent it. Why get yourselves involved? He isn't even trained."

Don't these people know? Have they not heard? There is a religious standard by which man relates to his fellow man. "All men are brothers." "He who honors his fellow man honors God." No religious person — no Jew — can dispute this.

Don't these people know? Is it possible that no one has told them? Don't they understand that what the prophets proclaimed years ago is still true today? "Have we not all one Father? Hath not one God created us?"

The segregationist, avowed or latent, may not know this. But we Jews do. We have always been a people with an inspired sense of justice. And we have been too much a part of history not to know. We have felt the unjust sting of discrimination. Jobs have been closed to us. Schools have been closed to us. Neighborhoods have been closed to us. And good men, presumably good men, sane men, thoughtful men still harbor these very feelings!!!

Others may not know this, but we do. We Jews do! We understand that even the law is not enough. The law tells us not to injure. The law forbids us from denying others their rights. But religion goes beyond the law. It demands that we help! Judaism demands that we help the less fortunate, that we protect his liberties, that we enhance his rights.

It is not enough for us to applaud or even support Civil Rights legislation. Judaism instructs us to do more. It tell us to take the needy into our employ! It tells us to train him for a job! That's what Judaism tells us! Oh, it may be expensive. It may be less efficient for a time. But it is a religious duty! It is right! And it is imperative! For no community, no city, no nation can long endure so divided — half affluent, half despairing.

Man's Relationship to God

The third factor of religion is man's relation with God.

How shall man relate to his God? "We know," says those politicians who want to breach the wall separating church from state. "We can tell you. You pray. You may not pray at home. You may not pray in church or Temple. But, at least, your child will pray at school."

What should man do? "We'll tell you," they say. "Your children should listen to the Bible. They may not understand it. It may be a Bible different from their own. But it will have the school's stamp of approval. And if they do not want to listen, if you do not want them to listen, they are free to leave the class."

How should man feel? "It's simple," they say. "Let's have an amendment! Let's change the Constitution. Let's really make religion important."

I have devoted my life to religion. God is my guide. Prayer sustains me. How I wish this value and this truth could be imparted to all men. But don't these people know? Have they not heard? Virtually every major religious group in this country has opposed such a constitutional change.

Don't these people know? Is it possible no one has told them? Don't they understand that what the prophets taught years ago is still true today? "When ye make many prayers I will not hear" (saith the Lord). (Just) "cease to do evil, learn to do good."

Those who want a constitutional amendment may not know this, but we Jews do. We believe in God. We worship the King of Kings. But the proof of every thing we say, of every thing we believe, is in the deeds that we do, not the prayers we utter.

And we have been too much a part of history not to oppose such an amendment. We know that religion must be a private matter. We know that true religion is not dependent on governmental decree, public school programs or slogans. We know that no man can be truly free if in any manner his religious

9

convictions are regulated by the state!

Judaism Gives Us Direction

These are political issues — these issues of which I have spoken: the John Birch Society, the enforcement of Civil Rights and the proposed amendment to the Constitution. The candidates will make much of them. They are religious issues, too, for they affect our well being, our beliefs, our way of life. And the people of this nation have it in their power to decide. We will have to make decisions about them, you and I, for these are issues invisibly written on the ballots of next November. Where can we more confidently turn for guidance in making these decisions than to the precepts and principles of our faith? Where can you and I more assuredly search for direction than within the framework of our religion? And Judaism — Judaism confronts these issues forthrightly and directly. It points the way for us without equivocation — without question! It directs us to repudiate the Birch Society and those who carry its support! It directs us to stand against all who, in any manner, shun the responsibility of making Civil Rights real! It directs us to oppose all who would change the Bill of Rights and thereby jeopardize our religious freedom!

Tomorrow Needs Our Help

The year that faces us will be a trying one. Of this we can be certain. The election — no matter which party wins — will not stay the fervor and ferment now begun in the land. And here once more religion and politics meet. The campaigns look to tomorrow and to the future. They look to the promise that political platforms pledge. And religion looks to the future, too. Religion is founded on faith. It is built on hope. It is certain there will be a tomorrow and that it will be better than today.

"Tomorrow needs our help." Our religion says to us, "Tomorrow needs our help. We can make it what we want, you and I. A little effort and it yet shall be."

Tomorrow *does* need our help. The future *is* in our hands. We *can* make it what we want. You and I, and the millions who look to their respective faiths for guidance. And I pray that speaking above the political speeches we shall soon be hearing, testifying louder than the appeal of the John Birch Society, pleading more earnestly than the claims of those who oppose Civil Rights Laws, producing more logic than the politicians who would change our

Constitution will be the still small voice of religion, spurring us to noble thoughts and nobler deeds, urging us to bring a greater tomorrow to our country, to ourselves and to all men, wherever they may be.

May we find this in our power to do, O Lord.

Amen

* * * *

Death Teaches Life
September 15, 1964

Somewhere in Boston, perhaps at this very hour, my mother and my brother and sister are gathering for a Memorial Service. Not too far away, in another Temple, my other brother is standing, just as I am, to speak to his congregation. And he, just as I, comes in a dual capacity.

They are there, as so many of us are here, because our hearts are sad. We have suffered losses which cannot be replaced. Whether those we loved passed away recently, or in months or years gone by, their presence has brought us here. And we come together for another reason, subconscious though it may be. We are here to acknowledge before God that we are only human, that we realize we do not control our destinies, that we are well aware of a Power beyond us Whose hand touches our shoulders — Who bids us live and Who beckons us to die. And we, you and I, who mourn, have a special closeness. Just as my mother and sister and brothers are bound to me by our own bereavement, so are we all bound together. All of us who have at some time grieved are bound together with a feeling that those who have not experienced death cannot now know.

I, as you know, am well acquainted with Death. I thought I knew it well, for I have seen it often. I have stood with a young man in the morgue of University Hospital as he looked for the last time at a wife whom a surgeon's skill could not save. I have brought the news of children's deaths to shocked parents. I have seen the old die and the young, the infirm and the healthy. Oh, I am well acquainted with Death. Everytime someone I know dies, everytime the voice on the phone says, "My wife, or my father,

11

my husband, or my mother just died," I know Death better — and I die a little too.

I thought I knew all about Death. But I didn't. Not until last February when my own father died. I shall never forget that telephone call — the urgency in my brother's voice. I rushed home to Boston, despairing at delays, silently urging the planes to fly faster, praying that all might yet be well. And then — then I was in my own house of mourning.

I have entered many homes that are in grief. Far too many. Far too many times has my heart broken as I have seen the tears you shed. Far too many times have I asked with you, "Why, God? Why?" And far too many times have I had to steel myself to try to give the calmness, the comfort, the strength you sometimes needed to weather the shock. And now I was in my own house of mourning. My own father was dead!

Somehow I knew that my brothers and sister looked to me to bring comfort to our mother. They had been at her side those past hours when my father's life had seeped away. They had spent themselves to no avail. Maybe I, coming from afar, could bring strength to their weakness. And I did comfort my mother. All her children were now gathered about her. And I showed such strength, such restraint. I shed not a tear that Saturday nor even that Sunday, when we sat through the funeral, listening to my father being praised as a gentle soul, as a learned man, as a "lamed vavnick" — one of the 36 righteous men who according to Jewish tradition walk the world for humanity's sake. I did not shed a tear even when my father's teacher, the 86-year-old Rabbi and scholar who taught him Talmud, came to my mother with eyes overflowing.

Only once did I have difficulty. And that was at the cemetery. "Say something for us all," my mother pleaded. "Dad would want you to say something for us all." And so standing at her side I said, and it was not my normal voice, "I remember saying 'goodbye' to my father once before. I was ten years old, and I was going to camp for the first time. I thought I was a big boy, and I did not know whether to kiss him or to shake his hand. And so I shook his hand. But I know better now. Ever since I became an adult, I have known better. And now, for all of us, I kiss him goodbye."

Soon the period of mourning was over and I had to leave. I had to return to Minneapolis. And my mother stood there at the door, so sick, so thin, so little. And she was now waiting to say goodbye. It was then that I cried. Nothing could hold back the pent up tears. I cried. I cried the tears I have seen you cry so many times. And she comforted me. As a mother always comforts her child, she comforted me.

I have thought about the week in Boston many, many times. For you see, my father's death had a meaning for us that his life did not have. We learned so many things we knew to be true, but which we had never spoken about. We learned, just as all of you must have learned when your dear ones died, what was truly lasting and meaningful about his life. We learned that the gentleness of his being had touched every heart, that his love for learning had aroused every respect, that his honest humility had blessed all who knew him.

How many times have I said to you that the spirit does not die? How many times have I repeated this at Services? Now for the first time I learned what it meant, just as I am certain you have learned. We sat and talked about our father in death as we never had in life. And we still do. We compared him with men whose pride overshadows their achievements, and we praised him for what he was to us. We marveled at how he had struggled to send us all to school, and we admired him for his quiet accomplishments as we never had shown in life. We recalled his gentleness, his humor, his love for us, and we loved him as we never really had expressed in life.

I, who come to this Memorial Service, am a mourner just as you. I weep in my heart just as you. And I can approximate now, for the first time, how you who have lost a life's companion must weep. I do not know the hurt, I cannot know the loss, but for the first time I can truly understand. But I understand, as never before, something else. I now know that my father is not completely gone — nor are your dear ones. I think of him more often now than I did in the past. Every time I say Kaddish I think of him, and should you see a smile on my face when I begin to recite it, you will know that some pleasant memory has touched me.

And as I think of his life, I muse to myself: How I wish I could be as gentle as he, as considerate as he, as understanding as he. And I think of the wonderful statement of the rabbis "Zecher Tsaddik L'vracha — the memory of the righteous is for blessing."

13

How true. Our dear ones, now gone, have given us blessed memories. They have shown us life — a life that is now completed. They have shown us by their being that which is good in life. They have given us perspective, understanding, and a heart that knows what comfort can bring. What greater blessing can we leave those who will remember us? What greater treasure? What greater inheritance?

And so, though we meet in memory, we meet also in thanksgiving. Yes we do. For we say in our hearts, "Thank you, God. Thank you for these lives. Thank you for our loves. Thank you for our dear ones, who in life sustained us and who in death, bless us."

Zecher Tsaddik L'vracha . . . for, you see, the memory of the righteous *is* for blessing.

Amen

My Eight Congregations

From time to time we have had a "New Members Sabbath" at Temple, and to it we have especially invited the individuals and families who have affiliated with us over a year's time. It is a Service of welcome, and of course, there is a sermon.

"My Eight Congregations" was one such sermon. Though I could now add one or two other "congregations" that have emerged since I first wrote this sermon, it appears here as it was originally given.

* * * *

As you can see from our Service program, we call this evening the New Members' Sabbath and I — on behalf of all of us — the rabbis, cantor, Walter Baron, officers and members of our Temple Board of Trustees, our office staff, the entire Temple family, want to especially welcome to this Sabbath those of you who have become a part of Temple Israel this past year.

As I am sure you know, we are a relatively large congregation, but we want you to feel that it is a small one. We want you to feel that this Temple is yours, that you belong, that you are needed. We want to know you individually, to have you feel at home here. And we try in many ways. Sometimes we succeed, sometimes we fail. But we continue to try — and you can help us.

Let me tell you what one of our new members did some two months ago. She called me. "Rabbi," she said, "my family is new in town and we have just moved into a new home. Would you come and put up our mezuzah?" So one Sunday afternoon Bernice and I came. I put up the mezuzah with the appropriate blessing and we spent a pleasant few hours getting to know the family.

"What made you call me?" I asked her over a cup of coffee.

"Well," she said, "We are with a large company and have been transferred a number of times. I discovered that if you want to get to know the rabbi, you have to make the opportunity." And it was a delight for us and, I think, for them to share that opportunity. So we are available to you. We look forward to knowing you. We hope you will get to know us.

You who are new among us, and perhaps many others who are here, may think that you joined only one congregation when you affiliated with the Temple. It isn't so. There are actually eight different congregations, all here, all under one roof, all known as Temple Israel. Let me tell you about them.

My first congregation is our Concentrated Congregation. This is the congregation concentrated in our Temple directory. These are the names that make up Temple Israel! Twice a year — as you who make choices between a 5:00, a 7:00 and a 9:00 time know — twice a year it concentrates at a Service. And there most of this congregation, I like to deceive myself, receives instant inspiration and enduring religiosity, for it does not — by and large — reappear for fully twelve months when it harkens once again to the call of Kol Nidre.

How else do you explain the strange phenomenon of such membership? About 3,500 individuals come to our Holy Day evening Services. Where do the bulk of them vanish thereafter? I assure you, and I can assure them, that by and large the sermons are better during the year, that the music is as uplifting and the liturgy as inspiring. But my guess is that very little will help. These members of our Concentrated Congregation concentrate on one thing only — getting a place in this Sanctuary on Rosh Hashanah and Yom Kippur. And even though they suffer, and we suffer, by their rare appearance, I confess that I am grateful that they come at least those two times — though I still do not know whether I should be flattered that we give such long-lasting sanctity in so short a time; or be concerned that we drive them away for so many months by what we say or do those fleeting evenings.

* * * *

My second congregation is my Crisis Congregation. This is the congregation that needs the Temple, or the Lord — or calls upon the rabbis only when a crisis of some kind occurs in their households. The telephone rings. "Rabbi, you may not know me," says a voice. "My 17-year-old daughter is pregnant and she is not married. We have been to counsellors and social workers. We have been all over, but she wants to keep the baby. She is not now and never will be competent to care for it. You just have to do something."

The telephone rings. "Rabbi, my son is dating a girl who I

16

know is just not good for him. Will you talk to him?"

The telephone rings. "Rabbi, my parents quarrel all the time. I just can't live in that house anymore. Please help them."

The telephone rings. "Rabbi, my child was in an accident", "my son was picked up by the police", "my wife has run away and I don't know where."

Calls such as these can come in from the members of all our congregations and any of us who receive them are eager to be of help at any time and in whatever way we can. But what makes the calls from my Crisis Congregation different from all the others I receive, is that its member never see or speak to me until a crisis arises — and then they do not see or speak to me again until the next crisis appears.

* * * *

There is a third congregation — and though I do not have the figures, I think it is our largest. This is my Kiddie Congregation. These people join so that their children may get a Jewish education. These people join because they hope their children may find here a sense of the spiritual, a feeling of belonging, or a direction to their beliefs. But though I do not see many of its members very often on Friday evenings, it is nonetheless a congregation in which I place much hope. For by bringing their children to us, these members want to preserve Jewish life. Their trouble is that they themselves often do not know how — and are almost never here to find out.

As you know, children learn best by imitation. They learn from their parents. We, at Temple, are a poor substitute for the home. That is where Judaism begins — that is where the training for Jewish life starts. Without it no synagogue could exist. All we can do here is to strengthen what your homes provide. We can give a Jewish foundation academic rooting. We can help it to flower. But we can never fully do all this with the child alone. The family must participate.

The hope of the members of our Kiddie Congregation can almost never succeed if the congregation is limited just to the kids.

* * * *

There is a fourth congregation — my Confined Congregation. It is relatively new and it is growing. It is the congregation of the nursing home, of the long-care hospitals, of the homes for the aged. Sometimes its members do not leave their own homes.

I love this congregation. I love to see each of its members. And I think they love to see me.

But I do not see them often. Time and distance are almost forbidding. Sometimes I just call them and their joy relieves my weariness. Sometimes I merely drop them a note.

I appreciate greatly when someone calls me to tell me of a new member in that congregation. All you have to say is "Rabbi, my mother — or father — or give me a name — is in such or such nursing home" and I will make every effort to get there or to inform our Sisterhood Visitation Committee.

And I must tell you — my Confined Congregation is my most understanding congregation — and my best teachers — for though I am saddened each time I visit, in most of them I find a fortitude and faith that strengthens my own.

* * * *

There is a fifth congregation — my Cavalier Congregation. This is an unusual congregation. I sometimes wonder why they have joined us. Sometimes I think they have become part of this congregation because its building is impressive. Sometimes, I suspect, they join because it may be good for business, or they may anticipate the need of a rabbi for a funeral or a wedding.

How do their conversations with me run? "Rabbi," they say when I see them at some function or at a lecture or at a concert — for it is never at the Temple. "Rabbi," they say with a knowing smile, "I haven't seen you for a long time." Or, "Rabbi, that Temple of yours is becoming Big Business."

Fortunately the membership of my Cavalier Congregation is very, very small. Once I was greatly upset by them. I thought the fault of their feeling was in us. Now I know that it is basically in them. I would frankly like to woo them into one of our other congregations, but I get no chance. They won't let me. They proclaim their minds are open to all truth, to every new idea, but they have shut them to things Jewish and refuse to disturb the closed membership.

To the man who smiles as if there is a sacred secret between us as he proudly declares he has not seen me for some time, I often reply, "Well, you know where I am every Friday evening."

And to the man who complains that religion is just big business — that the Temple is always looking for money, I say, "Unfortunately we do need money. I wish we did not. But we do."

And I sometimes continue with something like this: "Do you want Judaism and Jewish life to simply waste away? Do you want your grandchildren to be Jewish? Then perhaps you should be contributing to the Temple even beyond what you are now giving. The Temple cannot be maintained by hope, by history or even by full congregations on Friday nights. You belong to many things. Which one is more important for the future of Judaism than the Temple? You give money willingly to many causes — Jewish and general. Why is the Temple lowest on your giving priority?

* * * *

Then, I have a sixth congregation — my Constructive Congregation, and I appreciate it no end. It is a congregation whose members will send me the program of a Temple they may have visited elsewhere. Its members feel free to suggest to me ways in which we may improve our services to you. It is the congregation that calls me when a distant relative of one of our members may have passed away, or when they know someone is in a hospital I normally do not visit.

Our Constructive Congregation is the one that participates in almost everything we do. Not only is it here on Friday evenings, but it enjoys our study groups, our Sisterhood and Men's Club.

And our Constructive Congregation has helped shape our Friday evening and Sabbath morning Services; it has helped us be creative and all for the good of the Temple.

I long to hear from more of its members. For how else do we know whether we are doing all that we can, in the best way that we can.

* * * *

There is a seventh congregation — a wonderful congregation — this is my Concerned Congregation. Its members are concerned with everything. They are concerned about Jews and Judaism. They are members of the ADL and Hadassah, and Brandeis and

ORT, of B'nai B'rith and Mt. Sinai Association. They give time and money to the Council of Jewish Women, the Federation, the Community Center. They work for Jewish Family Service. And they do not limit themselves to Jewish causes. Everything that affects humankind may be part of their purview — politics, schools, the United Way, Big Brothers. They are involved, in their own way, in making our community the best possible community for us, our children and our children's children. Some are very often in our Sanctuary; none, if any, ever fail us when we call upon them. I like to think the Temple stimulates them toward many of their interests.

I have but one slight fault to find with the members of this congregation. For a goodly number of them the Temple, the synagogue in general, is just another aspect of Jewish life and is no more important than any other institution engaged in important Jewish activities and concerns. Their prime loyalty to Jewish life can be through Jewish culture, or the State of Israel, or the Ten Commandments or through struggling against bigotry. They sometimes fail to see that the source of all Jewish living is here. They sometimes fail to see that there is nothing else — no other agency, institution or formula — dedicated to the perpetuation of our faith and people.

* * * *

Finally, there is my eighth congregation — my Committed Congregation. It has everything my Concerned Congregation has — and more. This congregation looks upon the synagogue as the most necessary ingredient for the advancement of Judaism and Jewish life. This congregation finds in Reform Judaism the most vital and the best possible means of living as a Jew in our American environment. This congregation is committed to the Temple as to no other institution. It appreciates its teachings, it understands its values, it knows its demands. To this congregation prayer has meaning and Jewish knowledge is essential. And all of this is rooted in a deep and abiding faith in God.

When I think of my Committed Congregation as it relates to the seven others, I think of a parable I once read:

A man took a seed and planted it in the rich soil. The sun shone on it and the clouds rained on it. Soon it brought forth a rootlet and a leaf; a bud and a flower. Then the man plucked the flower from its root and after it withered, he dissected it, burned it, and weighed the ashes. He wrote a learned paper describing the perfume of the flower; telling of the atoms it contained and the waves of light it absorbed and reflected. And other men, on the basis of his study and knowledge, and the substance that was the flower, tried to make it live again. But they failed. Only God can do that!

And so it is with many of us and Jewish life. We dissect it into many parts — philanthropy, Israel, defense work, education, cultural values, and ethical teachings. We analyze it in the test tube of scientific findings. We weigh it against the secular interests of modern life. And when we try to assemble these elements and make them into a viable design for living, when we try to conjure them again into the fragrance, the color, the beauty of Jewish life, we fail — for it cannot be done without the synagogue and God. For my eighth congregation — the synagogue and God are central.

*　*　*　*

Well, these are my eight congregations. Some members of Temple Israel belong to two of them, some belong to three, others four or five. Which will you, who are relatively new to us, join? They are all available. They are all here for you to partake of. Which ones will you join? And may your choice bring blessings to us all.

Amen

The Ron Edwards Case:
The Use and Abuse of Power
February 23, 1968

One of the tasks I took upon myself when I became a rabbi at the Temple was to become actively involved and to involve the Temple, as an institution, in the struggle for Human Rights and Civil Liberties.

Almost immediately, I began to speak on the subject, and over the years, when the times were explosive and the struggle dangerous, I devoted many a Friday evening to analyzing the tensions, attempting to articulate the Jewish position and trying to point out what our personal stance had to be. No other matter — not even the Vietnam war — was as disruptive.

Our congregation responded magnificently. We were the first congregation in the area to have a Social Action Committee, to teach a course in Black History, to send a delegate to walk with Martin Luther King on that historical march in Washington. We were the first congregation to resolve not to trade with any business that discriminated in its hiring practices.

I personally was appointed by Governor Levander to serve on the State Commission Against Discrimination. I was a founder and served as a president of the Minnesota Council on Religion and Race. I was a member of the Minneapolis Committee on Fair Housing and was appointed by Mayor Naftalin as a delegate to the organizational meeting of the National Urban Coalition. I became a member of the Board of Directors of the Minneapolis Urban Coalition and was the chairman of its Police-Community Relations Committee, a very challenging task in those difficult days. I was one of the ten Minnesotans appointed to represent our State at the funeral services for Martin Luther King, Jr.

But perhaps the most satisfying of all my involvements was the Ron Edwards case. It came in the wake of rioting and burning in North Minneapolis.

When the "case" was resolved, the **Minneapolis Tribune** *did a series of articles on it. Rabbi Rutman wrote a paper on it for one of his PhD courses at the University. The* **American Jewish World** *published a front page story headlined "Rabbi Shapiro, Temple, Sparks Drive to Confirm Edwards".*

Here is the sermon I gave on February 23, 1968. As you read it, you will again note that the word "black" had not yet come into our vocabularies as a term of general use.

* * * *

It is not often that I change a sermon topic after it has been announced in our Temple Bulletin. Actually it has happened only once before. In October, 1966 I had planned to preach on the subject "The Bible — Hollywood Style" and had prepared a sermon comparing the movie that was then showing with the Hebrew text. On the Friday that the Bulletin appeared indicating my subject for the following week, there was a panel discussion here at Temple called "The Negro in Minneapolis." Some of you may recall it. Remarks were made by one of the panelists that were not only erroneous but could well have been interpreted as malicious and anti-Semitic. Everyone who was present was disturbed and aroused. I felt that some response had to be made and during the days that followed I met with that panelist, confronted him with the issue, and elicited an apology. I felt it necessary to bring the results of that confrontation to you. And "The Bible — Hollywood Style" was never preached from this pulpit.

Something similar has happened in the past ten days and for the second time in my rabbinic career I have changed a sermon topic after it has been announced. If some of you are here to listen to "What Difference Does It Make — We're in Love," the topic I was scheduled to discuss this evening, please forgive me. I shall speak on that subject on March 8.

The Ron Edwards Case

This evening I want to discuss the Ron Edwards Case and to tell you why I felt my discussion of it could not wait.

For those of you who may not know the issue, let me touch on it very briefly. There is within the governmental structure of our city a Mayor's Commission on Human Relations. It is to be comprised of fifteen members all of whom are appointed by the Mayor and confirmed by the City Council. In December of last year, Mayor Naftalin submitted his fifteen selections, among which was Ron Edwards, one of three blacks appointed. Fourteen of the names were confirmed by the Council. Ron Edwards was not. The reason given by those Council members who voted against the confirmation was that Edwards had a police record.

Now I know that there are many details that I have not mentioned. I know that there may have been political overtones and crosscurrents and that there are accusations on all sides of the political spectrum. But it is not with politics that I am concerned.

The fact is that the Mayor did submit the name of Ron Edwards. The fact is that Ron Edwards does have a police record. The fact is that Ron Edwards is representative of what might be called the moderate to militant element in the Negro community. The fact is that the Council did not confirm him. It was the Mayor's prerogative to choose Edwards. It was the Council's prerogative to refuse to confirm. This is incontrovertible.

But the matter does not and did not end here.

The Council's Action

The Council's action had a jolting effect on the Minneapolis Black community — a jolting and cohesive effect. Like all communities there are many factions in the Black community. There are so-called "Uncle Toms." There are conservatives. There are moderates and militants. But the rejection of Edwards by the Council brought them all together. On this issue they spoke with one voice.

They selected leaders to represent them to the Council — not militant leaders, but men responsible, understanding and highly regarded by the white community. While this representation was being made, the two other Negroes who had been confirmed for the Commission, the Indian member and a number of the white members declared that they would not serve until the issue was resolved.

The Negro community felt affronted and humiliated. It was not Ron Edwards as a person whom they supported. Many did not know him. Many felt there might have been better representatives. But he now became a symbol of the white community's indifference to the needs of the Black community.

Hoping that the response of the Black community had stirred the Council, the Mayor resubmitted Edwards' name. Once again it was rejected.

While the Negro community seethed, the leaders whom it had chosen attempted time and again to break the impasse. But the Council majority was adamant. At one point, however, its leadership offered a compromise. It proposed that the ordinance be changed and that the Mayor be permitted to appoint the 15 members of the Commission without Council confirmation. The Black community refused. It wanted Edwards confirmed.

The Present Standstill

This is where the matter stands. The Black community asks that Edwards be confirmed. The majority on the Council will not vote to do so. Whatever else has taken place before is now immaterial. There is a direct confrontation. There is a standstill.

Though to some members of the City Council, the case of Ron Edwards was closed, it remains an open wound to the Black community. The militants are now vying for the position of leadership in the Negro Coalition. The militants are now saying "You moderates, you conservatives, you Uncle Toms, you can get nothing from Whitey. He just laughs at you. All he understands is rioting. All he understands is violence. That will get us what we want. It always has. And if it doesn't, at least we will show that we are men, not lackeys."

During all this many of us in the white community were indifferent. Some did not care what happened. Some thought the confrontation would pass away. Some thought it all political shenanigans. But a great many — perhaps the majority — secretly and even openly exulted. "The Negro got theirs," they said. "This will show them. They can't push us around. If they get tough, we can get tougher." And they applauded those Councilmen who had rejected Edwards.

Meanwhile continued efforts were being made to have the Council reconsider its position. The Board of Directors of the Minnesota Council on Religion and Race, of which I am chairman, passed such a resolution. It asked the Council to confirm Edwards in the name of justice and for the welfare of the city. Unknown to us, a group of prominent businessmen had come to the same conclusions.

Some ten days ago, one of these men, Mr. Wayne Thompson, a vice president of the Dayton Company, approached Bishop Hamilton Kellogg of the Episcopal Church. "How could the Business Community join with the Clergy," he asked, "to effect Edwards' confirmation or to find some reasonable solution to the problem?" Bishop Kellogg suggested that he come to see me in my capacity as chairman of the Minnesota Council. And thus began a week of meetings, telephone calls, statement writing, and activities such as I have never experienced before.

The three of us, Bishop Kellogg, Mr. Thompson and I met, and decided to call a meeting of interested business men and the Board of the Council for Thursday of last week. We came together at 3:00 p.m. that day here at Temple. All the businessmen Mr. Thompson had called were present. I shall mention just a few. Mr. John Cowles, Jr. of the Minneapolis Star and Tribune, Mr. Raymond Plank of the Apache Corp., Mr. Wayne Hoffman, President of Bell Telephone, Mr. John Moorhead, president of Northwest National Bank, Mr. Paul Parker, Vice President of General Mills, Mr. Dean McNeal, Vice President of Pillsbury. Among the clergy were Bishop Kellogg, Bishop Cowley, Bishop Nall, Dr. Perron, the president of the Minnesota Council of Churches and representatives from virtually all the Protestant denominations. We formed an Ad Hoc Committee of concerned citizens. Mr. Thompson and I were appointed co-chairmen.

All of us were of one mind. In the name of justice and for the sake of peace Edwards had to be seated. Two committees were formed: A Contact Committee to speak to the Mayor, the Councilmen and the Negro leadership; and a Statement Committee, to formulate some statements of policy and to develop a petition to the City Council.

A Business-Clergy Coalition

The next morning at 8:00 a.m., our Committees met for breakfast at the residence of Bishop Cowley to crystallize our thoughts. Most of the day was spent on the matter.

At one point during that day, Mr. Thompson and I met with some of the leaders who had been serving as spokesmen for the Black community. We learned a number of things. But above all, we learned that unless the moderate Negro leadership could gain some success with the white power structure, it would be totally repudiated. "The City Council has let us down," said one of the Negro leaders. "They affronted our integrity. They undermined our influence."

On Saturday afternoon, the Ad Hoc committee met at Temple once more. Reports were made. Some Council members had indicated they might change their positions. Others seemed to listen more attentively than ever before. Labor leaders had been contacted and were showing concern. An informal poll, taken by one of the major businesses, showed that the citizenry was becoming more aware of the true issue. And then we formulated a statement asking the Mayor to resubmit Ronald Edwards' name to the Council and calling upon the Council to confirm it.

Monday there were more meetings. This time with a political figure asking him for advice: His answer: "There has to be a groundswell of public opinion. Councilmen have to hear from people in their wards. Members of the community have to make their voices heard, have to sign petitions, have to move some of the members of the Council from their rigid and callous position, even though it seems to me that what is right is right no matter what one's constituents say." My response was to call a hasty breakfast meeting of clergy for yesterday morning. Some sixty clergymen came. I suggested that they go to their congregations, as I was going to mine, to rouse them to the danger of the situation and to place before them the moral imperatives inherent in the case.

What I Believe

Now, I know all the objections to Edwards. He is not representative of all the Negroes. He has a criminal record. Men of such character should not be honored with a responsible position. His appointment indirectly affirms lawlessness. Then why do I believe that he should be seated on the Commission? Why have I spent so much time and effort?

I believe Edwards should be confirmed because it is just. He has a criminal record, it is true. But he has paid his debt to society. He is now employed in responsible work. Do you believe that someone who has sinned can never be forgiven? Do you believe that someone who has broken the law should never have the opportunity for leadership? And do you know what our tradition says about this? Do you know what Judaism says? "The penitent, the individual who has done wrong and repents; the individual who has done wrong and begins to live a responsible life, he is more worthy than the person who is perfectly righteous."

I believe that Edwards should be seated because it is right. Often men must make a choice between two rights — or two sets of principles if you will. "It is right" the Aldermen may say, "it is right to refuse to seat Edwards because he has a criminal record." "It is right," I would respond, "that the Negro community have the representative it suggests sit on a public body constituted by and large, to protect its welfare." Here are two rights. Which is the greater one? Which is the more pertinent principle? I would choose the latter — the greater right is for the Negro to have representation.

For the Sake of Peace

I believe that Edwards should be seated for the sake of peace. We must either recognize that the Negro community is part of American society with the same drives and motives as the Jewish community, the Irish, the Swedish, the Italian or we classify it as second class. We either must bring the Negro into the general community, must open it wide for him or we deliberately create two nations in this country. We either accept the Negro community where it is — and not in our own suburban image — and try to help it by improved education, work opportunity and better living conditions or we must be prepared to accept conflict as a way of American life.

I believe Edwards should be seated for the sake of peace. Every national Negro leader, the President of the United States, governors, mayors, the advisors to our Federal Government, all tell us there will be trouble in American cities this summer. I do not know whether there will be violence and rioting in Minneapolis, but I can tell you this. If there is, the fact that Edwards was not seated will be a contributing factor, and indirectly the Council must be held responsible. We had an opportunity — I believe we still have an opportunity — to change that course, but it is in the hands of our Council and in the Mayor's Commission on Human Relations — if there ever will be such a Commission in our city.

And that is why I changed my topic for this evening. Time is short. Black people have used their power and abused it. They turned to violence. The Minneapolis City Council used its power and abused it. It would not listen to the voice of reason.

Now you and I must use our power. We must use our influence. I know that the men on the Council are capable of reassessing their position. We must show them that this is not only what we want — but that we want it because it is right!

The Statement

The statement our Ad Hoc Committee developed is, in part, as follows:

> It is obvious to many of our citizens that Minneapolis faces a serious crisis and significant opportunity in racial relationships. The challenge revolves around the appointment of Ronald Edwards to the City's Commission on Human Relations. After a serious evaluation of all the factors involved, we believe that the Minneapolis City Council should confirm the

appointment of Mr. Edwards.

In urging this approval, we believe that the goal of justice is inherent in the concept of American democracy and is one of the tenets of the Judeo-Christian Heritage.

NOW, THEREFORE, we the undersigned:

1. Request the Mayor to resubmit Ronald Edwards' name for confirmation to the Commission on Human Relations.
2. Request the Council to ratify this appointment.

Men of good will are signing this petition all over the city. Sheets for your signature will be in the Temple office and in the foyers. Avail yourself of the opportunity. On Monday we shall gather all the petitions and present them to the Council.

An Appeal

I ask the Council to reconsider its position. I ask it in the name of reason and righteousness. I ask it for the welfare of our city. This is no time for recrimination but for restitution. This is no time for jingoism but for justice. This is no time for polemics or for politics, it is a time for peace.

I pray God that we may have it — if not in the world, at least in Minneapolis.

Amen

*   *   *   *

(Following this sermon, and those by other clergy, and after a meeting with the leadership of the Council, the Mayor submitted Ron Edwards' name once again and he was confirmed.)

A Letter To The President

Almost every year, for the past ten years or so, I have written an open letter to the President. I have given it as a sermon from our pulpit and then have sent it off to Washington. The response does not change, although the administrations do. There is a form letter "thanking me for my concern."

Here are two complete letters — one to President Ford, the other to President Carter — and an excerpt from the first letter I wrote to President Carter after he insisted upon being called "Jimmy."

* * * *

October 11, 1974

Dear President Ford:

It has been my custom over the past years to write an open letter to each new President soon after his assumption of office and I do so now with many concerns and great hope.

You know, I am sure, that all our hearts go out to you and your dear ones at the sudden and serious illness of Mrs. Ford, and we pray that she will soon be returned to perfect health. And, of course, you know that you have our full support in your efforts to conquer the dangerous economic conditions of the country. I am not an economist, nor do I fully understand all the implications of your proposals. I do know, however, that laws continue to exist which provide great corporations and numerous individuals with tax loopholes and dodges while placing maximum burdens on those who can least afford it. That, you will agree, is unfair and unconscionable. Certainly some change is imperative here.

But the economy is not the purpose for my letter. I am concerned with other matters — matters in which I have more competency to write.

Piety and Religion

From all I have read and seen, Mr. President, prayer is very meaningful to you. You pray at public worship. You pray with a small group of friends. But all of us are more aware than ever before, that prayer and worship can be a facade and that there is a vast difference between piety and religion. Your predecessor was consumed with piety, with the observance of ritual and rubrics, but he was not a religious man.

And because I am a rabbi, because I am concerned with the moral tone of our country and its leadership, because I feel deeply that decisions affecting our lives must be rooted in ethical conviction, I respectfully wish to offer to you some religious insights and perspectives that come from Jewish tradition.

The Nixon Pardon

First — the pardon of Mr. Nixon.

The pardon, as you are well aware, did not close the matter as you had hoped. Much has been written about your decision, much more will be written, and the question of equal justice to all and mercy for some will be debated for many months.

I personally was stunned by your action. It is not that I am not forgiving. Nor is it that I am not compassionate. We Jews have an entire Holy Day given over to forgiveness and compassion. Again and again, in our liturgy, we read of God's lovingkindness and His desire to forgive. But that is not all. Our Holy Day is called Yom Kippur, the Day of Atonement. God's forgiveness — and our forgiveness — is tied to contrition. We are told that we must understand our offenses, and acknowledge our sins, before God's pardon for us — or man's — can be complete.

As you know, Mr. President, this has not been the case for Mr. Nixon. As a matter of fact, his daughter, Julie, has had the audacity to suggest that her father become a roving Ambassador, representing our country abroad. What an affront to our moral sensibilities, no matter how capable he may be! What an indication that the Nixon family is even now unaware of his offenses against the nation, against our democratic system, against untold individuals and against us. How can the moral strength of our country be maintained when offenders are rewarded? How can we endure when compassion dominates to the exclusion of justice?

The rabbis of the Talmud tell us that God created many worlds before he fashioned the one in which we live. None of them seemed suitable. He created one where only justice prevailed. But no human being could exist in it. Life was much too rigid and harsh. So he destroyed that world. Then he created a world where mercy alone prevailed. And soon corruption and crime were everywhere. All offenses were pardoned, all guilt absolved. Anarchy was the rule. So God destroyed that world as well. Finally he created our world — a world where justice and mercy were to reside side by side, where justice is tempered by mercy, but mercy does not jettison justice.

Crime in the Land

There is another matter I would call to your attention, Mr. President. I have noted your great concern with the continual rise of crime in the land. The *Minneapolis Tribune* some weeks ago quoted you as saying "We must take the criminals out of circulation. We must make crime hazardous and costly. We must insure that swift and prolonged imprisonment will inevitably follow each offense. Only then will we deter others from pursuing careers of crime."

It is not my intention to place those thoughts of yours within the context of the Nixon pardon, but rather to indicate to you that Mr. Elliot Richardson, the former Attorney General, holds a completely opposite point of view. In a speech before the Amicus Society last month he contended that studies made by his Department showed that swift and prolonged incarceration was not the answer to crime.

Perhaps a Jewish insight might help. Rabbi Meir lived in Talmudic times, some 2000 years ago. He was greatly disturbed by crime and criminals. On one occasion he became so distressed that he prayed for God to punish them all. When his wife heard his prayer she was astounded. "No where in the Bible does it say 'Let sinners be destroyed in the land' " she chided him. "But it does say 'Let sin be destroyed.' Instead of praying for the destruction of the sinner, why not pray for the destruction of the conditions that cause sin."

Mr. President, in all honesty, is that not the best method of controlling crime? To attempt to create conditions where men and women would not resort to it. To provide adequate education, prideful work, honest incentive, proper compensation. To maintain and improve the social program initiated some administrations ago.

A Too Strong Presidency

A further concern of mine, Mr. President, stems from a recent article entitled "A Too Strong Presidency" written by the eminent historian, Barbara Tuchman. Let me quote from it.

"If there is one lesson to be learned from Watergate," she wrote, "it was the danger in the overuse of the executive power. Within a month of taking office, President Ford made these disquieting remarks, indicating a swelling sense of personal absolutism. 'The ethical tone will be what I make it . . . In this situation I am the final authority . . . My conscience says it is my duty . . .' ".

I am certain, Mr. President, that absolutism is not in your character but it may well be inherent in the office of the Presidency. Again may I offer a Jewish insight.

Do you remember the story of David and Bathsheba? If you recall, David, the King, wanted to marry Bathsheba, the wife of Uriah, a captain in his army. So David contrived to have Uriah sent into battle and be killed. After a time given to mourning, Bathsheba became David's wife.

And then Nathan, the prophet, appeared before the King. "There is a man in our kingdom," he said to David, "who had but one sheep. And he was the tenant of a man of immense wealth with many flocks. One day there came a visitor to the man of wealth and he desired to prepare a feast for his guest. But he did not take a sheep from any of his personal flocks for the feast. Instead he took the one sheep from the man who was his tenant. What shall be done?"

"That man must surely be punished," cried the King. "Where shall we find him?"

"Thou art the man," said the prophet.

Mr. President, our Jewish heritage tells us that there is an ethic higher than that of kings. There is an ethic higher than the laws of Congress. There is an ethic higher than the ethical tone of presidents, no matter who they may be.

The Amnesty Issue

"My conscience is my duty," Barbara Tuchman quotes you as saying, Mr. President. And I agree with you. An individual's conscience is sacrosanct and personal. It does prescribe one's duty and one's actions. But if that is so, how can we as a people — and you as the president — agree to punish those individuals who because of their conscience would not fight in a war they deemed — and which we all now recognize — to be immoral and absurd.

For your Amnesty Program, Mr. President, though it does extend the hand of reconciliation, is also beset by intricacies and inadequacies, by unintentional inequities and injustices. I do not wish to detail all the objections I have to it. I just want to point up another insight from the Talmud.

A man once came to a Rabbi. "My government," he said to him, "has ordered me: Go and kill so and so. If not we shall execute you. What shall I do?"

The Rabbi answered, "Let yourself be put to death rather than commit murder. His life is no less valuable than your own."

I submit, Mr. President, that the conscientious objectors faced a similar situation, and many left the country rather than acquiesce to an order they found immoral.

Or perhaps the story from the Book of Exodus is even more direct. You recall how Pharaoh commanded the midwives to kill all the male children born to the Israelites. You recall how the midwives disobeyed their king's unjust command. And you recall what the Bible says thereafter, "God dealt well with the midwives." He rewarded them for following the dictates of their conscience.

Mr. President, it is not my intentions with this letter to criticize or to be unfair. But in Jewish tradition even God's actions can be questioned and argued. You are said to be a religious man and this gives us all great hope. I pray that your prayers and your actions will reflect the religious imperative at its very best, and that these few insights from Jewish values will help guide you in these troublesome times.

May you be granted the strength and the wisdom so desperately needed.

Sincerely,
Rabbi Max A. Shapiro

* * * *

April 28, 1978

Dear President Carter:

I have written to you a number of times this past year, but the letter I write now is a public letter. I shall read it to my congregation and all others who are present on Friday, April 28, before I send it to you.

Some months ago I wrote concerning my visit to the White House to thank you for the opportunity to be part of a briefing on the Panama Canal treaties. I must tell you that I was greatly impressed with the briefing, with your understanding of the problem and with your logic and skill in presenting a solution. It was, in my estimation, a significant display of leadership. I congratulate you and our entire nation that the treaties have now passed the Senate.

These days, however, your leadership is in question. The polls indicate that public approval of your policies is dismally low and the press — local, national and international — cite you for indecision, vacillation and lack of understanding of the complexities that confront your office and administration.

I know, Mr. President, that I am not competent to give advice on the multitude of issues you face daily. There is one issue, however, on which I believe I am relatively able. I write to you about it now, and I write with a deep sense of disappointment. That issue is peace in the Middle East and the security of the State of Israel.

Campaign Promises

Mr. President, I am well aware that campaign promises are often forgotten once the oath of office is taken. Many people in politics say much for expediency and promise much for the sake of votes. You, however, led us to believe that Jimmy Carter's word was good, that he was not the ordinary candidate for office; that morality and character were his stock in trade and that honesty and justice and, perhaps, even love would characterize his administration. But from my perspective, it has not been so. Certainly not in the search for peace in the Middle East.

I have researched some of the statements you made during the months before the election of 1976. Let me mention only one. In Boston, in October of that year, you attacked the Ford Administration's sale of weapons to Saudi Arabia and you said: "I see no reason to sell arms to Israel's enemies." These words have a hollow and even terrifying ring to them today.

They ring hollow because you now propose to sell 60 F15's, one of the most sophisticated air weapons in our arsenal, to that same Saudi Arabia.

They have an aura of terror about them for, to me, at least, they indicate that you have submitted to the power of petroleum and, perhaps unwittingly, to evil.

The Odyssey of Mark Segal

I have been reading the odyssey of Mark Segal, who recently resigned as one of your administrative assistants. I have before me the story of his appearance last February before a young leadership meeting of the United Jewish Appeal. At that time he loyally defended with all the vigor and eloquence at his disposal, the proposed sale of the F15's to Saudi Arabia. The nearly 800 people present responded with boos and hisses when he told them that the F15 was a largely defensive interceptor with limited aggressive capabilities. That is the information he had received from the National Security Council. That is what, in all honesty, he repeated to the United Jewish Appeal group.

I suspect, Mr. President, that you are aware that Segal repeated another lie to that audience. He told it that the air base the Saudis were building at Tabuk, some 150 miles from Israel's southern border, was an ordinary airport. And again he was booed. But that is what he had also been told by the National Security Council.

As I understand it — and there has been no denial — when Mark Segal, shaken and upset, returned to the White House that day, he telephoned the Defense Department to check his facts. This is what he was told: First, the F15 is the world's best fighter/bomber with considerable offensive punch, capable of delivering up to 15,000 pounds of explosives to any target. Second, Tabuk was a major military base being built with U.S. assistance.

In an interview with the *Jerusalem Post*, your former assistant declared that he felt he had been deceived and that he thereafter refused to defend the administration's Middle East policies. His resignation followed. As you know, it has been called a "resignation of conscience," the first of its kind in Washington in many years.

Saudi Arabia and Israel

I do not know why Mark Segal, who was your formal liaison with the American Jewish community, was deceived. Nor do I understand why you have repeatedly said that the sale of F15's is not a threat to Israel and that "Saudi Arabia has never been actively engaged in any aggression against Israel."

Did you realize, Mr. President, that as early as 1948 the Saudis furnished a battalion of troops under Egyptian command for the invasion of the newly created State of Israel? Did you know that Saudi forces were in Jordan in 1967, ready to attack Israel if King Hussein gave the word? Did you know that in the Yom Kippur War several Saudi soldiers were actually taken prisoner by the Israelis?

I am sure you cannot read all the press, Mr. President, but let me quote to you what Saudi leaders have been saying. Said King Khalid to the *New York Times,* "When we build our military strength we have no aims against anybody except those who took by force our land and our shrines in Jerusalem — and we know who that is."

Said Defense Minister Sultan to the *Christian Science Monitor:* "All our weapons are at the disposal of the Arab nations and will be used in battle against the common enemy."

And Foreign Minister Saud assured *Newsweek:* "In time of war, when the interests of our brother Arab nations are involved, (we will use) whatever resources we have to hurt our enemy." And the resources — some $15 billion of armament and equipment which this country has already sold to Arabia — and billions more in oil wealth.

It is obvious to me, as it must be to your advisors and to you, Mr. President, that with the base at Tabuk and with the vast Saudi military buildup, that Saudi Arabia is becoming a new confrontation state with Israel. And it must also be obvious that the 60 F15's will be used — should, God forbid, another war occur — if not by the Saudis themselves, then certainly by one, if not all, of the other hostile countries that surround the Holy Land. Who can guarantee that it will not be so?

Other Questions

There are other questions I would ask for your consideration, Mr. President. Did you know that last year alone, Saudi Arabia provided the PLO with 28 million dollars? I am sure you are aware how that money is used. Since 1973, Israeli settlements have been bombed more than 1,500 times and over 100 Israeli men, women and children have been killed because of them. Explosives have been placed in Jerusalem busses, at the Hebrew University and other public places. And the last terrorist attack on Israeli civilians was called "courageous" by the Saudis.

Did you know that among the weapons recently captured from the PLO in Lebanon, the Israelis discovered an array of standard United States arms and explosives, all bearing Saudi markings and serial numbers. And it is not merely against Israel that the PLO operates. In the past 10 years, there have been 865 so-called "actions" in 20 different countries.

I assure you, Mr. President, that I do not agree with all the Israeli Prime Minister Mr. Begin has proposed, said and done. But there is one final question, one essential question that is at the core of all I have written. I know that you are vitally interested in peace in the Middle East, as we all are. I know you recognize Israel as the only democracy in that part of the world, as we all do. I am sure you know that it is the one stable, unwavering ally that this nation has had in that vast area, that an Israeli peace delegation is still in Cairo and that negotiations for a settlement have not been completely abandoned. I know your concern about our dependence on oil from Saudi Arabia and the turmoil that a possible boycott might bring. And my question is simply this: How can the sale of weaponry at this moment, how can a confrontation with Israel on the one hand or with Saudi Arabia on the other, hasten a Mideast agreement or even enhance its prospects?

Does it not seem that these are the wrong sales at the wrong time? Could not this be a blunder that will destroy all that President Sadat's initiative began? Is it worth taking the risk? Why do you insist?

The Words of Isaiah

I know you read the Bible, Mr. President. Perhaps you recall the words of the prophet Isaiah, who wrote some 2,700 years ago at a time when there also was tension and hostility between Israel, Egypt and Assyria. Isaiah wrote: "The day will come, saith the Lord, when . . . Israel will be the third with Egypt and Assyria, a blessing in the midst of the earth (and He will say) 'Blessed be Egypt, My people and Assyria, the work of My hands, and Israel Mine inheritance.' "(19:24)

It was a promise of peace, Mr. President. A promise that someday Egypt, Assyria and Israel would join to be a blessing to themselves and to each other.

That promise I know you can help fulfill, and I pray God that you will — but it can never come by jeopardizing Israel's borders and its people.

Sincerely,
Rabbi Max A. Shapiro

*   *   *   *

March 18, 1977

Dear Mr. President:

I know that you prefer to be called Jimmy, but I doubt whether I shall ever be able to address you that way. I am, of course, very conscious of what has been termed "your style." I applaud the way you have deflated the royal pomp and pretention that had gradually encrusted the presidency. I appreciate your desire to be one of the people, but I respectfully suggest that you are not. You have been selected by us to be the most important person in the land, and though you are one of us, you are nonetheless apart from us. You are the only person who can touch our collective souls. You, more than any other human being, can affect our collective destiny. Your judgements, your sensitivity, your manner shapes the mode of our society. I want to be able to expect greatness from you. I want to be able to manifest pride in you. I want your office to have an aura and an awe to it. I want to regard the president of my country not as anyone better, but as someone special. So I shall call you "Mr. President." For, indeed, that is what you are.

Religion's Most Difficult Question
November 9, 1979

"Theology" has not been the ostensible core of my preaching. Rather, I have attempted to let my beliefs, and the Jewish imperative as I saw it, pervade everything I did.

Nonetheless, there were many occasions when I spoke on a matter primarily theological. "The Meaning of Israel," "The Chosen People," "Rabbi, Give Me Faith," "Three Views of the Messiah," "A God in Which to Believe" have been subjects which I had addressed. Here is a sermon I gave on November 9, 1979 — "Religion's Most Difficult Question" — why must there be tears and sorrow and suffering.

* * * *

In my 25 years in the rabbinate I doubt whether I have ever experienced a week such as the one that has just passed. I remember two heartbreaking funerals in one day — and the names may be familiar to you — Max Rappaport and Harry Hartstein, but never has there been for me four funerals in six days, each special, each emotionally exhausting. Never has each night of a week begun with a Shivah call. Never has there been the responsibility of a sermon following so hard upon difficult days and evenings.

At first I thought I would forego a talk this evening — that I would say to you, "it has been impossible for me to give the thought and writing time to an effort that would be worthy of you as a congregation." But then, in the past days there have been calls from congregants who have apologized for not being able to be present this evening and asking for copies of what I would say. And I am prideful enough to believe that there may be others who have come just to hear what our Temple newsletter said I would talk about.

For the question I want to pose with you is unquestionably religion's most difficult question. Why should there be suffering? Why should the innocent suffer? Why should a baby be born blind; why should a young, beautiful wife be wracked with cancer; why should a young mother or father die; why are there boat people; why starvation not only in Cambodia but in other parts of the world; why Hitler and crematoria? If there is a God why does He allow such misery? If religion is to make sense, how can all this torment be?

A God There Is

That there is a God is obvious to me. I find no difficulty — despite the suffering — in such a belief. It is a matter of faith. And I define faith as believing in something one knows to be true but cannot prove. I do not know whether I will be alive tomorrow; I cannot prove it this moment, but I have faith that I will. I do not know whether I will arrive home safely after this Service. I cannot prove it now, but I will get into my car and drive off with certainty. I have faith.

But it is more than that kind of faith that gives me my belief. I am awed at the order in the Universe. What would be if light did not travel at the same rate of speed every time? What would be if the earth did not move around the sun the way it does? What would be if tomato seeds did not produce tomatoes, or chicken eggs did not produce chicks? What kind of chaos would there be? Could life exist?

And I am awed at what I feel — seeing a helpless newly born grandchild some weeks ago, wondering at the wonderment of how he came to be. I am awed when I see you — what a magnificent being each of us is. I am awed that there are billions upon billions of cells in our brains — in a small object that weighs only some four pounds — and that each cell has a function and interacts with other cells perfectly. I am awed at poetry and music, at television and airplanes, at skyscrapers and pyramids. I am awed at a rose; a weeping willow tree; I am awed at love. Where did it all come from, this ability, these feelings, this creativity, this beauty?

And because of this I can rationalize some of the suffering. God, this Creative Intelligence in the universe, this Instiller of feelings, this Orderer of stars and planets, has given us free will. He has granted us the dignity of shared power. He has given us the freedom to do good — and also to do evil. And when people choose to be cruel and barbarous, one to the other, misery is the result; starvation is the result; degradation is the result.

Some years ago in Philadelphia a snow laden telephone pole crashed on the car of a passing motorist. The driver was injured and sued the telephone company. In defense, the company claimed that such an event was beyond its control — that a snow storm was an "Act of God" and therefore it was not liable.

The court ruled that inasmuch as the company had not inspected the pole for a goodly number of years, the company was negligent and responsible and ruled against it.

That's how it is with us. God permits evil by granting us freedom. But He does not give us His permission to be negligent or so willfull as to injure or destroy another of His human creatures.

Natural and Physical Laws

And I can rationalize the suffering caused by nature. Each year we read of deaths caused by earthquake, tornadoes, storms, avalanches, forest fires ignited by lightening. Why if God is good, should it be? Doesn't He have control? What kind of God is that?

And yet we know we live in a universe subject to natural and physical laws. What would it be like if the force of gravity was different in California than it is in Minneapolis? What would it be like if chemicals mixed together ignited in one instance and did not in another? What would it be like if the speed of sound was unpredictable; if scientists could not understand disease; if clouds did not bring rain; if the physical development of a child into an adult were unpredictable?

If a universe of human freedom can produce an Idi Amin as well as a Mahatma Ghandi, an Adolph Eichman as well as an Albert Schweitzer, a universe of dependable natural law is also not in every sense under divine control. God does not create earthquakes, but he has created a world where the conditions for earthquakes exist.

The Basic Question

But still the basic question remains unanswered. Why must there be the dreaded and dreadful cancer? Why must the young die when there is so much for which to live? Why must leukemia ravage babies? Why does there have to be senseless accidents? Why? Why? Why?

Some Answers

If you think of it, there are a number of answers, though not one or any may be the total answer. There is an answer found often in the Bible and one which many people find plausible. It goes something like this: There is a purpose beyond our human understanding that gives sense to seemingly senseless events. That is the way God willed it. Our little minds, our limited intellect, just cannot comprehend. But we have to believe that there are reasons, and that there is meaning. We just have to believe. Period.

Then there are those who say that suffering is part of life — that all of us suffer, some more, some less. The rabbis of old acknowledged this rather well when they asked, "Is it better to be born or not to be born? With all the suffering in life is it better to be or not to be?" And they answered, "We do not know, but inasmuch as you are born, make the best of it." And how do we make the best of it? By the way we face what befalls us. The story of Louis Pasteur who was paralyzed at age 46 and who still continued to create and write, thrills the most insensitive of readers. The ability of Beethoven to compose though deaf, the brilliant achievements of Helen Keller, the fact that Franklin Roosevelt could rise above the shattering experience of polio, the people in our own lives who have confronted adversity with courage and a smile, have shown us what the human spirit at its best can do. They have given us an insight to what character really is. That, too, is an answer.

Then, there is the answer that suffering is punishment for the sins we have committed. That is so foolish a response that it is not worth comment. I mention it only because some misguided individuals somehow may be duped into believing it.

There is another answer — one that many of you may find as appealing as I do. It says that though God *could* eliminate all the suffering everywhere, He has created a universe controlled by laws, natural, physical, moral, and He will not and does not change them. God, says this answer, is all powerful, but He has placed limits on His own power.

God is like one's father this answer says. There are many things our fathers may want to do for us — or did want to do for us — but cannot or could not. A father cannot get you into medical school if you do not have the aptitude or the grades, no matter how much you wish it or he wishes it. He cannot shower you with wealth if he has none. He can't even take a driving test for you. But that does not mean he does not love you. That does not mean you cannot turn to him again for help or that you cannot depend on him. His heart may be broken by his lack of capability. There just are restrictions on what he can do or cannot do, despite his desires.

So much for answers.

The Need To Believe

I must tell you that for me who, from time to time, must face the suffering of someone I love or a tragedy in a life of a family I love, there is a time when any attempt at answers is almost obscene. There is a time when any and every answer is inadequate. Ultimately at moments such as those we have two choices: we can deny life's meaning or we can reaffirm our faith in the mysterious wonder of the universe.

Most people I have encountered at such times want and need to believe. The very question "why?" "Why did this happen?" bitterly though it may be asked, indicates such a need. They may even say "If such a tragedy can take place, if life is so unfair, there is no God." Yet despite their anger they live as if there is meaning. They may rail "If this can happen to someone so decent, so good, there is no point to decency and compassion." Yet they are not prepared to teach their children to be mean, to be selfish, to be uncaring, to be cruel. Nor are they prepared to live that way themselves.

Most people I know are the captives of hope; and hope is an essential part of our humanity. We may glibly speak of might triumphing over right, yet all of us yearn to celebrate the victory of right over might. We may speak stoically of a cosmos that has no moral base or purpose, but most of us — if not all, nourish the hope that in some way there is an abiding quality in the universe, a goodness, a meaning to our existence — that there is an immortal spirit within us.

Finally, what really matters as we go about our daily routine is what we do with our suffering. If we endure it with courage we can mature, we can grow and our painful journey through life can take on profound meaning for ourselves and others. I have seen such suffering. I have seen such a spirituality emerge. I have seen it encompass those whose lives have been touched by it. I have seen it create a greater compassion, greater sensitivity, deeper love.

* * * *

Judaism has always been practical in facing religion's most difficult question. The existence of God was always taken for granted. If there is injustice, if there is suffering, our tradition tells us, let us try to explain it as best we can, but more important, let us do something about it, if we can.

That may not be an adequate response for all of us, but it is a beautiful response — to help where it is needed; to give support when it is needed; to stretch out the hand of friendship and concern with kindness and hope.

Why there is suffering is a question that permits no simple answer. Each of us is bruised by the harsh realities of life. But, thank God, we can search for affirmation in the midst of pain; we can attempt to make of each trouble a blessing.

Grant that we do, O Lord.

Amen

THE FEDERATION AND THE SYNAGOGUE

You will note that there are five items in this volume that address Synagogue-Federation relations and particularly Temple's request to our local Federation for subvention of our educational programs.

I first raised the issue publicly on Rosh Hashanah 1974. However, my passing reference to it at that time caused such consternation among some of our congregants who were fearful that the Federation campaign would suffer and Israel be the victim, that I decided to clarify my position in the sermon, "The Federation and Jewish Education" (October, 1974).

From 1974 to 1976, our Temple Board held back from making a formal request to the Federation but tried to find an answer to our educational needs by an accommodation with the Talmud Torah. There were a number of meetings between us, all of which were ineffectual. In 1976, I addressed Synagogue-Federation relations from another aspect in my talk, "My Hopes For The Coming Year," but still little was done. The decision to ask for subvention was a difficult one for our Board to make. Finally, early in 1978, when we felt we had exhausted every avenue open to us, and with inflation certain to curtail the continued development of our Hebrew and Religious Schools, our Board of Trustees made our request.

In due time the Federation appointed a committee to study the matter. After some exploratory meetings with our Temple Committee, the Federation Committee asked us (1) to change our request of subvention for our entire educational program to merely the Hebrew portion of it, which we did; (2) to explore once again with the Talmud Torah the possibility of some accommodation, which we also did; and then it procrastinated. It sent a letter to the total Jewish population in the county, and without providing the facts relative to our request, asked that individual and personal judgements be made on its validity. It evoked anger, half truths, and specious declarations that polarized a community whose unity we all wanted to preserve.

Our Temple Committee, nonetheless, tried its utmost to be patient. Its members were essentially in two camps at the same time: ardent supporters of the Federation; and dedicated to Temple. The Committee that it dealt with, with the exception of the three Temple members who served on it, had a commitment to the Federation and to the Jewish educational system that had evolved in Minneapolis over the past years.

Our people could not bear to see the Federation — and that meant Israel — suffer; the Federation Committee was not as sanguine about Temple.

As negotiations plodded along I made three statements on the matter, and they are being reprinted here. Two of the statements were "Rabbi's Messages" and both were written to clarify and to inform our congregation as to what was transpiring. The first was written in response to the Federation Committee letter; the second, my statement to the congregation on Kol Nidre Eve, 1979, was an expression of my exasperation at the protracted delay by the Federation Committee; and the third is my initial reaction to a proposal the Federation Committee finally presented to us.

At this writing, discussions continue.

* * * *

The Federation and Jewish Education
October 25, 1974

As many of you recall, on Rosh Hashanah last, I spoke briefly about the Federation and its relationship to our Temple's Religious School. Some of you heard one thing that evening, some of you heard the very opposite. Some of you were highly pleased with what I had to say, some were greatly distressed. Some of you understood the context of my remarks, others completely misinterpreted them. Such are the imponderables of preaching.

I must tell you that I had hoped to provoke a reaction that evening and I was pleased, though surprised, that the response was so pervasive and widespread. I had hoped to open the door to a subject that must be faced candidly and forthrightly by every Jewish community in the country. I wanted to expose you to a matter that I believe will be one of our crucial issues in the next few years. I wanted this community to begin to think and to talk about the relationship of the Federation to the synagogues. You did, and I am most grateful.

Preliminary Comments

And this evening I want to expand my remarks of Rosh Hashanah. But first, a few preliminary comments.

1. The question of the relationship between the Federation and the synagogues is not a new one nor is it limited to Minneapolis.

This is a national issue. We, at Temple, have been talking about it privately for some time. Some two years ago, Marvin Borman, who was then president of the Temple, sent a letter to the president of the Federation, advising him that a request for a Federation subvention to the Temple's Religious School was a possibility, and that the matter was under consideration. A Temple Task Force was appointed at that time to look into it.

That Task Force is now meeting. It may decide to recommend to the Temple Board of Trustees that we seek a subvention for our educational programs; it may decide not to. The problems raised may be too great. But let me emphasize — to date the Temple has made no such request and has not been rejected. Some of you seemed to gain that latter impression from my Rosh Hashanah talk. Believe me, if such had been the case, my remarks would not have been as brief nor as placid. I would have tried to have blown the roof off the town.

2. What I say this evening is not meant to be critical of the Federation, though it is not sacred, and there is much that can be said. Nor shall what I say this evening fully express my thinking about the relationship of the Federation and the synagogues. That is a different, though tangential subject, and I leave it for some other time. What I am talking about tonight is what may well be an antiquated attitude of the Federation toward the totality of the Minneapolis Jewish community. Our Jewish community is not what it was when the Federation was formed. It has changed. Its institutions have changed. Its agencies have changed. The outlook of our people has changed. Their needs are different. Their concerns are different. Their demands are different. Just one example will suffice. In 1965 the Talmud Torah, considered the community school, had 1280 students. Today it has about 775. In 1965 Temple Israel Religious School had about 1000 students. It has in excess of that number today. The focus of Jewish education in our town has obviously changed. Our Federation has been progressive in many areas. But it can be mired into immutability by myopia.

3. I do not want anyone leaving this Sanctuary this evening with the impression that I am hostile to the basic purposes of the Federation. I do not want anyone to take my remarks as an excuse for not giving their utmost to the Federation Campaign. The needs of Israel are greater than ever before. Israel is in more danger politically and militarily than ever before. It is beset by

unprecedented economic difficulties. And should 60,000 Russian Jews seek haven there annually, the needs would be greater than we can now imagine. The Federation Campaign will soon begin. Your fullest support is required.

4. Nor do I want anyone leaving the Sanctuary with the impression that Temple Israel has hit upon difficult times. We are one of the great congregations in the country with a national reputation second to none. According to the Federation study of 1972, more than 1/3 of all the affiliated Jewish families in our community are members here. Our membership is strong, our Religious School larger than last year, our programs vital and exciting. And this evening I am not talking about Temple Israel alone, though that is the center of my attention. I am talking about Jewish education — all Jewish education, and that includes all synagogues and their schools.

5. Because of the nature of this talk, I shall be making references to the Talmud Torah and to Torah Academy, both of which receive financial support from the Federation. I want you to understand that I do not mean here to be critical of or to appraise their administration, curriculum, programs, or competence. All those are internal matters and far beyond the scope of this evening or my involvement.

A Matter of Principle

Now to the question at hand — the Federation and Jewish education. I shall talk about it from four perspectives.

The first is principle. As a matter of principle, should the Federation be interested in Jewish education? If so, what is its responsibility?

In Minneapolis, the principle of Federation involvement in Jewish education has long been established. It has financed what it chose to call a community school. It finances a bus system so that children can attend that school. I recall when taxis were sent to outlying areas to transport children who did not live near a bus route. All this in the name of Jewish education.

But if the Federation is truly interested in Jewish education, should not its interest extend to all children who might want to learn? The Federation is a community enterprise, concerned with the total community. Why must it limit its concern to particular schools?

Why must it be that if a family wants a Jewish education for its

49

children, our community, through the Federation, says in effect "We will help you but only if you enroll your children in the Talmud Torah or Torah Academy. If you do not, there will be no Jewish education for your family. At least none with our support. Or go to Temple Israel, it will support you."

Is this the way we want our community to respond? Is this our display of concern and responsibility? Or do we want every child to have an education, the kind of education suited to the needs of that child and its family? Do we not want every Jewish school to provide the best education possible for it? Do we not want to help educate rather than hinder; to bring in rather than exclude?

It seems to me, that as a matter of principle all Jewish education merits Federation support!

A Matter of Precedent

But it goes beyond that. There is also the matter of precedent.

For years the Federation has helped finance the Talmud Torah. That was its sole educational recipient. That was the one school that received community financial support. Last year, the Federation began to subsidize the Torah Academy, our local Jewish Day School. The reasons, as I heard them presented were: Torah Academy was serving a special segment of the community, it was teaching Torah, it was good for the community, it was in need. Whatever the reason for its actions, by granting Torah Academy subsidiary status, the Federation recognized that there was more than one Jewish school system in the city and that both were its responsibility. So a precedent was set.

The actual fact is that there are three — or more — Jewish school systems in our town. Temple Israel has the only other large and complete system, and we have more children enrolled than Talmud Torah and Torah Academy combined. The other synagogues have schools, too. Ours, however, is as unique in its approach as Talmud Torah is in its, or Torah Academy in its. Ours, too, services a special, and incidentally, a substantial segment of the Jewish population. It, too, teaches Torah. It, too, is good for this community. And, with inflation, it too, may be in need. With rising costs, it, too, may be in financial difficulty. What then? Where does it turn for help, if necessary?

"Oh," some people may say, "go to your membership. Get it from your Temple membership." How often do you think that can be done? And who can estimate what negative effect this may have on a Federation campaign?

"Oh," some people may say, "Temple Israel is not a community school. You are not open to everyone. One has to be a member of your congregation to go to your school." This is the kind of thinking that perturbs me. This is the kind of specious thinking that closes eyes to needs and change. This is the kind of antideluvian thinking that may destroy cohesive community efforts.

Do you know that a number of years ago Temple Israel's Religious School was open to the entire Jewish community? Do you know there was a tuition charge for non-members? Suppose now we were to open our doors again? Suppose now we were to go back to a tuition system for those who are not members? What would happen then to enrollment at Talmud Torah? Would it increase or diminish? And would Federation help support those children who chose the Temple school?

A Matter of Preference

There is not only a principle involved in Federation support for Jewish education, there is a precedent as well. And there is also a matter of preference.

Minneapolis is not a monolithic Jewish community.

As you well know there are three distinct Jewish orientations in our city. In many areas we are similar. In many areas we join together. But there are differences. And these differences cannot be ignored or glossed over. There are different approaches. There are different emphases. There are different traditions and rituals. We each have and do our own thing.

And that, interestingly enough, is the tone of our times. That is where the future is. The melting pot philosophy has given way to cultural pluralism. Differences are in. Black studies, Jewish studies, Chicano studies are part of campus life. In many public school systems kids have a choice as to the kind of school or curriculum they want. All of us, we openly acknowledge, cannot be fitted into the same mold, no matter how magnificent some of us may think that mold is.

Let me ask you: "Is there an authentic Jew? Is there one Jewish model after whom you would pattern your life? Is it Moshe Dayan? The Lubavitscher Rebbe? Golda Meir? Moses Maimonides? Theodor Herzl, Amos, Isaiah, or Moshe Rabenu? Who of us in a community as large and diversified as this can say, 'This and this alone is the Jewish education every Jewish child must have? This is the only way?' "

In our community as all over the country, the Orthodox group says one thing, the Conservative group another, and the Reform group still another. And every family should have the right to choose which education it wants. Every family should be given community support, if it needs it. And if that is our thinking, as I believe it should be, then fair-minded and community-oriented individuals can find means, through the Federation, to make it so.

A Matter of Priority

Finally, there is a matter of priority. What should be the priorities of the Federation? Israel, of course. Without us, Israel could not exist. It needs our material strength, our political strength, our energy, our prayers. That is the Federation's primary concern. But there is also the concern for a strong local community.

It seems to me that no matter what the Federation does or does not do, no matter how many agencies or institutions the Federation supports or does not support, there cannot be a strong local community if the synagogues are not strong. Without vital, vibrant synagogues, in two generations or three, there will be no Minneapolis Jewish community of any substance.

If we want Israel to exist we need Jews who want it to exist. No one else will be constantly concerned. If we want Israel to exist we need to educate Jewish children to know about Israel. We need to foster in them a love for the land. We need to give them a sense of relationship, a sense of commitment to it and the Jewish people! Where does this come from? Where does it come from primarily, if not from their Jewish education — from the schools that provide it. You know this as well as I. And that should be the basic local priority of the Federation. The schools! All schools! Not limited to one or the other! Every Jewish child must have the opportunity to obtain a Jewish education, and be helped in acquiring it by the community!

* * * *

Rabbi Alexander Schindler, President of the Union of American Hebrew Congregations, was in Israel last November just after the Yom Kippur War with some thirty leaders of American Jewry. On their last night there, they met with Golda Meir. "She was a bent and broken woman even then," Rabbi Schindler reported.

"She was bent in despair, and when she bade us farewell," he wrote, "she charged us in this unexpected manner."

"I do not tell you to give us more material help," she said, "because I know, you know the need for it, and it will be forthcoming. I do not ask for more political support in America, for I know that you will offer this too, and with an open heart and hand. I ask you to return to your communities and to strengthen your synagogues and your schools, for in the final analysis the struggle for Jewish survival will be fought, not only along the frontiers of Israel, but in every Jewish school, and in every Jewish house of prayer in the world."

For Judaism and the Jewish people to continue; for the struggle for survival to be won; the battle must be fought not only along the frontiers of Israel, but in every Jewish school and in every Jewish house of prayer in the world.

Let this be our purpose. Let this be our deepening local purpose. To strengthen each house of prayer, to strengthen every Jewish school.

May it be so, O Lord.

Amen

*   *   *   *

My Hopes For The Coming Year
February 6, 1976

As you can see from the title of this sermon, I am to speak with you about my hopes for the coming year.

Now there are all kinds of hopes that you and I can have. We have hopes for ourselves and our dear ones. We have hopes for our city, our state; for our country and the world. We have hopes for peace in the Middle East and the security and well-being of Israel. But this evening I merely want to talk about — and share with you — some of my hopes for our local Jewish community — and specifically in the areas of synagogue and Federation relationships.

Tension In Jewish Life

One of the interesting and disturbing facets of the American Jewish life is the tension that exists between the Federations and the synagogues. Perhaps you are aware of it; perhaps you are not. Every magazine article that analyzes them mentions it. Every rabbinic conference finds it a part of the discussion. When the Federations meet in convention, the result is the same.

Some weeks ago, Dr. Daniel Elazer, who is studying the phenomenon and who is visiting many communities to gather material, came to meet with the Rabbis in the Twin Cities. Though all of us present recognized the great achievements of the Federation and the massive help provided to Israel through it, there was nonetheless a general unhappiness and uneasiness about its place on the local scene and especially its relationship to the synagogues. We rabbis disagree on a number of issues, but on this there was unanimity.

In many communities the difficulty exists because the leadership of the Federation is secularly oriented and there is an overt or covert disdain for the religious aspect of Jewish life. In some communities the tension exists because there is an encroachment by the Federation on aspects of life once considered the domain of the synagogue.

In some communities there is a feeling that the Federation — with its fund-raising apparatus and approach — has appropriated the only game in town: Israel. Unquestionably this is now the major concern of the bulk of the Jewish population. Giving has become a must. Giving has become a badge of Jewish identity. Giving for some is a sense of fulfillment as Jews; and giving is primarily what the Federations want. The synagogue then becomes secondary, even peripheral to it. The Federations, knowing that refusal is impossible, knowing this is an effective way of reaching the community, ask the synagogues for help, and it is provided willingly. But resentment occurs because Federations never — as far as I know — demand that its givers support the synagogue as well.

In some communities the Federation has narrowed the agenda of the Jewish community to just three issues: Israel, Soviet Jewry, and anti-Semitism; and has, by its publications and organization, directed the Jewish community to an overriding particularism. Jewish concerns become the only concerns. Of course, the three issues — Israel, Soviet Jewry and anti-Semitism — are basic for us. But, in many ways, this ethic of particularity, this inwardness has begun to replace the religious value system that we Jews represent. The quest for truth, for brotherhood, for freedom, love and justice, the battle cry of the synagogues for centuries, has been shunted aside or muted. The question asked in the community is no longer, "What does the Lord require of me?" but, "Is it good or bad for Jews?"

Where Funds Go

In some communities funds gathered by the Federation are, through no fault of its leadership, sometimes distributed with few questions and little thought. I have heard this accusation before, but it was most recently leveled by Dr. Marc Lee Raphael, associate professor of history at Ohio State University. In an article in the November 28 issue of the *National Jewish Post*, he pointed an accusing finger at the United Jewish Appeal, one aspect of the Federations. I quote, "The uses to which these dollars — that is, the funds allocated — are put, often result in delicious ironies," he wrote. "It is more than probable that the Jewish aged in Israel receive much sounder and more comprehensive services than Jews in Miami or Los Angeles." And he continued, "Money is given to yeshivas in Israel, while schools in this country are often denied funds."

I bristle when I read something like that latter statement. I resent when part of my contribution — however minimal — goes to support institutions which link Reform Judaism with anathema, that regard us as outside the Jewish fold. I resent when my contribution — however minimal — is used to support institutions that teach discrimination against women, that will not join with other Jews in common Jewish projects and needs. I resent when funds that could be used to help our synagogue schools are given away for yeshiva education elsewhere.

There are some Federations that continue to function as they have always functioned despite changes in attitude and needs around them. Evaluations of existing agencies are made, successes and failures assessed, backs are usually patted, congratulations received. Thought is seldom given — it seems to me — to questions such as, "Is there a better way?", "Is there an alternative way?", "Is there an additional way to achieve what the agency is designed to do?"

Our Community Different

Fortunately, our community is different in many ways from so many others. Our Federation is not in the hands of secularists, and the issue here is not one of the synagogues versus the Federation. The issue is something we as a community have never — or certainly not recently — paused to grapple with. The issue is the substance and meaning of Jewish life and how best to foster and maintain it.

Synagogue And Federation

Perhaps you would like to know how we arrived at our present situation, how the tension I speak of developed. The Federation came about because it had to. In 1918, for example, there were 3,637 separate Jewish organizations in New York to serve an estimated Jewish population of 1½ million — an average of one agency for every 412 people.* Consolidation was imperative. Federation was a necessity; and in time the Federation began to assume responsibility, not only for social planning, but for the administration and direction of welfare planning funds. In 1932, local Federations joined together to form the Council of Jewish Federations and Welfare Funds for greater cohesiveness and efficiency. Fifteen years later Israel became a state. Immigration, war, terrorism, became part of its life. Vast, unprecedented sums were needed and the task of the Federation became more important and more meaningful and more pervasive.

Federation as Community

In time, the Federations took on an aspect of community. Synagogues had their particular membership and ideology. But the Federation was an umbrella. It reached out to every Jewish household — if only for funds. It sought out every Jew, regardless of synagogue affiliation or none. And soon those agencies it supported and funded were considered community agencies. They got their budget in toto, or in part, from a central source of Jewish resources. They were community sponsored. Those institutions that the Federation did not fund were considered sub-communal or extra-communal. So community centers were part of the community. A Talmud Torah was community. But a synagogue or a synagogue school was not. It made no difference if synagogue memberships were three, four, five times that of a funded agency. It made no difference if it served more Jews than the funded agency, it was still not part of the community.

---

*Statistics based on an address by Rabbi Harold Hahn, Cincinnati, Ohio.

Soon the synagogues became defensive. They had been the central instrument in Jewish life for centuries. They had set the goals for the Jewish community. Their role seemed to be threatened by a new communal structure that was extracting money from the community, leaving relatively little for the synagogues; and with that money establishing programs of education and culture that the synagogues had been maintaining and felt they could do better, if only they had the funds.

Where Are We Today

So that is where we are today. Both institutions are here to stay — the synagogue because it is the essential source of Jewish life and existence; the Federation because Israel's needs will undoubtedly continue.

And the time has come, it seems to me, for these two major organized forces in Jewish life to begin to rethink their role, their place, their cooperation. And this is one of my hopes for the coming year.

I suggest — I call upon the leadership of the Federation to define for itself and with the rabbinate and synagogue leadership what is meant by community and a community institution.

I suggest — I call upon the Federation leadership to think in terms of serving the Jewish individual, rather than the Jewish institution.

I suggest that the time may be at hand to abandon the concept of one facility to answer the needs of all the people — of one school for everyone, one camp for everyone, one leisure time program for everyone, one counselling service for everyone.

I suggest that it is just as proper for community money to support a youth activity — be it USY or Temple Youth in a synagogue environment, as it is in a community center. I suggest that it is just as proper that community money be used to counsel families and children, to provide programs for the aging and aged in a religious environment as it is in a non-religious environment. And I suspect that more people would partake of the opportunities and profit from them.

Jewish Education

My contention is that if Jewish education is a priority of the Jewish community, then the question we must ask ourselves is not, "How do we fund a Jewish school?", but, "How do we provide for the Jewish education of every child in the community?" I suggest that rather than ask its funded educational agencies to solicit children from other schools, as was done here recently, that the Federation help to strengthen the existing schools. I suggest (as I have so often in the past) that if it is proper to provide funds for one type of Jewish education — or two — then it is proper to provide funds for all.

Rabbi Samuel Dresner, a well-known Conservative rabbi, a member of a task force of the Council of Federations and Welfare funds dealing with Federation and synagogue relations, had this to say in a recent article in *Opinion* magazine:

> It is time that the Synagogue speak with one voice: Federation's funds must go to the synagogue schools as well as to others . . .
>
> Let us consider a voucher system whereby each child would receive an amount in accordance with the kind of school he attends, or a per capita system whereby each school would receive an amount in accordance with its hours and the size of its enrollment.

I believe that is the direction in which we should be heading. I believe the synagogues should not be forced to go to the Federation for subsidy. I suggest that the Federation, in its social planning, be innovative and daring. I suggest that it seek out the existing educational facilities and actively attempt to provide them with whatever is necessary so that every Jewish youngster may have a Jewish education — one of his choice — and within that choice the best that can be provided.

It seems to me that if we want to reach the largest number of Jewish individuals for whatever purpose, then the avenue is through the synagogue. It is here they affiliate. It is here they are known as individuals. It is from here that we can reach out to them. And for this the cooperation of Federation and synagogue is essential. But it cannot be a one-way street.

Hopes For The Future

I have many hopes for this congregation in the kind of service and help it can be to our membership. We need a social worker — or another rabbi trained in that discipline. We have 114*individuals in our New Horizons group.** We have some 30 shut-ins — people in nursing homes or confined to their own home. We have

---

*150, in October 1980.
**for members, 55 and over.

single-parent families, men and women who have recently lost their mates, or who have been divorced. They and their children may need support, comfort, help. We have families with problems, we need closer communication with those who convert. There is premarital counselling, marriage counselling, divorce counselling. We have college students; young people searching for companionship. There are individuals with a variety of special needs, and they do not generally gravitate to the communal agency. They come to the synagogues and, even if they do not come to us, we can at least identify them. We can search them out, we can go to them. But where is the personnel? Where are the funds?

How I would like to offer a Reform day school — in the best tradition of the best private schools — to this community. How I would like to move Confirmation to the 12th grade, making the 10th grade merely graduation from Religious School. How I would like to send all our Confirmands to Israel for a summer. All this takes finances. All this takes teachers who are with us on a full time basis. How exciting it would be if a far-sighted Federation, interested in maximizing Jewish life, would say, "We can provide seed money for such projects. We want to help."

As you can see, I have many hopes — and I have merely expressed a few — or perhaps you could call them dreams. And they are not only for the coming year. They reach out into the future, the future of our Temple, the future of synagogue/ Federation relationship, the future of our community. If together we could think the problems through constructively, we might even be a model for other communities throughout the country.

Perhaps I am hoping for too much. Perhaps the dream is unattainable. But you know the rabbinic philosophy. It isn't up to us to complete the task, but it certainly is up to us to begin. Hopefully, we shall. God willing, we shall.

Amen

* * * *

Statement on Federation

September 30 (Yom Kippur), 1979

I have been very ambivalent about what my sermon should be this evening. There has been an urge in me to talk about our

Temple's request for Federation funding for our educational programs; to tell you where matters now stand; where they seem to be going; and to express my feelings and hopes. Unquestionably this is the forum and this is the place.

But this is also Kol Nidre Eve. For me this evening is a time for contemplation, not controversy; for reflection, not reproof; for introspection, not indignities. So this is the place, but this is not the time. The matter, however, has become most public and needs some kind of perspective. So let me just make this short statement. There will be more at a later date.

Our request has passed through a much too labored process. Our committee — or should I say, negotiating team — has been patient, flexible, circumspect, understanding. No real progress has been made, and I am greatly disappointed.

I have little quarrel with the Federation as an agency. What it does for Israel and in other areas is superb. And it has a process. That it has subverted that process in this instance, and has made our Temple, this great congregation, a community football, is an insult to each one of us and detrimental to it.

I have no quarrel with the Talmud Torah. It has a fine reputation. It is, however, a school that primarily serves a Conservative community. We have met with its people many times, and all of us realize, they and we, that it presently cannot and will not make the changes we must have.

I have no quarrel with those who suggest that the Federation supported schools — the Talmud Torah and Torah Academy — re-examine their programs. I go one step further. I suggest that the Federation re-examine its program for Jewish education, how it relates to every school, where the students are, what it is they need. That really, if you stop to think of it, was the nub of our request. That is what the Federation committee could have done, should have done. With goading perhaps, its chairpeople may now move in that direction. However, we cannot wait for such a procedure to be initiated, debated and resolved. Time is running out.

But there are some quarrels that I do have.

I quarrel with short-sightedness and parochialism. I quarrel with obtuseness, timidity, and lack of creativity. The Federation has exemplary leadership in other areas, but in the field of education it is mired in the past.

I quarrel with a Federation educational leadership that vocally proclaims its interest in Jewish community education, but by its actions shows little concern for the education of every Jewish child in the community.

I quarrel with a Federation leadership that either does not read, or completely ignores the recommendations that come to it from its National Council, recommendations outlining avenues for new synagogue-Federation relations.

I quarrel with those who raise the spectre that a subvention to Temple education means a cleavage in the community. That is a specious and spurious argument, a red herring, if you will. Ours is an excellent community. It is, I believe, mature enough to manage disagreements, and strong enough to integrate anything that is legitimate and proper and right. And our request is legitimate, proper and right. In the long run, its acceptance can only strengthen the community.

Our Board of Trustees made its initial request to the Federation over a year and a half ago. Two weeks ago, our Board made another request: this time, that the Federation give us a final answer by November 15. We have waited long enough! We have been patient long enough!

When we know the Federation's position regarding Jewish education, whether it is interested only in the education of children from Conservative and Orthodox homes, or is also interested in your children and grandchildren, when we know the Federation's position regarding Jewish education, then we will know what we — as a congregation — must do. We shall keep you informed.

*   *   *   *

RABBI'S MESSAGE

Temple Israel "News" — December 18, 1979

On Yom Kippur Eve I made a statement concerning Temple's request for Federation help for our Hebrew School Program. At that time I said the Federation Committee had been asked to give us some idea of its thinking by November 15. Whether our impatience spurred the Committee to action I do not know, but on November 10th we received a proposal from it that indicated much thought.

The committee's proposal is just that, a proposal. It neither approves or disapproves a subvention. It suggests that we reorganize our Hebrew School as an educational entity separate from the Temple. This has positive possibilities; it also has negative aspects. It may be acceptable; it may not be. We shall be considering it most carefully.

But whether or not we accept the proposal is not the end of the matter. The action of the Federation Committee will not automatically make the Hebrew School a beneficiary. The issue must then go to the Federation Executive Committee which may make other suggestions and then to the Federation Board of Directors. We have no idea what the outcome will be there.

So the end result of our request is still many weeks — if not many months — away. Meanwhile the Federation campaign continues. There is no question that Israel and local agencies need our help, and we just must not let them down. But we, at Temple, are also in need of funds. Without such we cannot continue our education program, even at its present level.

It was Hillel who put it as best as possible over two millenia ago. "If I am not for myself who will be for me," he said. But, "If I am for myself alone what am I, and if not now, when?"

As ever,

Thanksgiving or Gratefulness
November 24, 1977

Each year eight "downtown congregations" come together on Thanksgiving morning for a combined Service. The first such Service was held in 1947 with Plymouth Congregational Church, Hennepin Methodist Church, Westminster Presbyterian, the Cathedral of St. Mark's Episcopal, and Wesley Methodist Church participating. In 1967 Temple Israel and the Co-Cathedral of St. Mary joined with them, and in 1977 the First Christian Church was added to our union.

Prior to 1962, Temple had participated in a similar Service which was then held on the evening before Thanksgiving. Congregations in our immediate neighborhood — St. Paul's Episcopal, Lake of the Isles Lutheran, Adath Jeshurun Congregation, Trinity Baptist, and Grace Presbyterian — came together. For reasons that I do not recall, these Services were discontinued. I do remember, however, that attendance at them had become very minimal.

At present, our combined congregations meet in a different building each year with a different clergy as the preacher. In the years Temple has been part of the consortium, we have hosted the Service twice, and I have been privileged to speak twice. The following is the talk I gave at Plymouth Congregational Church on Thanksgiving, 1977.

* * * *

This is a special occasion for those of us in the religious institutions that comprise this joint Thanksgiving Service. For this is the 30th anniversary of when all this first began.

Thirty years ago, members of five of the eight congregations here represented — Plymouth, St. Marks, Westminster, Hennepin and Wesley — came together for a Service in this very building. Ten years ago, the Co-Cathedral of St. Mary and the Temple were added to the union, and this year — through the efforts of Dr. Frank See, the First Christian Church has joined us.

Life In 1947

I do not have to tell you that life in 1947 was vastly different from what it is today. Though the war was more than two years over, many of us had but recently been separated from the armed forces and had not really found our ways back into society and the economy. Hubert Humphrey had just become the mayor of Minneapolis and the first breaths of a liberalizing attitude began to pervade the community. Stereotypes and prejudices that had previously prevailed and had been taken for granted began to break down. I suspect that, in 1947, the Temple and the Basilica (as it was then called) could not have been invited with any ease to express thanksgiving with the other five congregations on a morning such as this.

But prosperity was everywhere. Jobs were available. The colleges and universities had expanded their programs for the veterans. Hitler had been defeated. Future wars seemed impossible. For most of us, God was in his heaven, and all was right with the world; or if it wasn't, it soon would be. We would all somehow find our niche with Him and in it.

If ever there was a time for thanksgiving, that was it; and you and I could easily recite the litany of things for which so many of us were thankful then, and have been over the years: home and family and friends; freedom and opportunity; comfort and material well-being; the right of spiritual expression; peace. I suppose I could try this Thanksgiving morning to re-evaluate all or some of these, and report to you how thankful we all should be that they are still ours. But that not only would be superfluous, it would be condescending. And, besides, thankfulness is not what I want to talk with you about this Thanksgiving Day. I prefer to talk about gratitude.

You see, there *is* a difference.

Thanksgiving and Gratefulness

Webster tells us that thankfulness is "an acknowledgement of a kindness or of a favor or benefit." "Thank you, ma'am," says the clerk when you purchase something. "What do you say to the nice man?" asks the mother to her daughter after you have given the child a lollipop. "Thank you," she responds automatically.

But gratitude is something different. The definition is "a warm and friendly feeling toward a benefactor prompting one to repay the favor." Those are the keywords — "prompting one to repay the favor."

Let me be personal if I may.

Sometime late in September, I had a telephone call from Senator Wendell Anderson's Washington office. After the initial

64

amenities, there was a question. Would I come, at my expense, to the White House for a briefing on the Panama Canal treaties?

Now I am sure I need not tell you that the call came as a complete surprise. My first reaction was "The Panama Canal treaties — why me?" Were it Israel or the abortion issue or energy — or some problem in which I was intensely interested, I would have known how to respond immediately — but to this I just said, "I will have to call you back."

Yet, as I thought about the call and discussed the prospect of going to the White House, my interest and excitement grew. How often is one invited to be with the President — in a small or large group — for I had no idea how many were being asked. So I called Washington, gave my social security number and birthdate for identification, as I had been directed, and waited for the next step.

A second call from the Senator's office finalized the trip; I made my reservations and at 7:40 a.m. on October 12 I was off to Washington. Twenty-seven other Minnesotans had also been invited.

We were met at the Washington airport and driven to the Senate Office Building for lunch and a meeting with Senator Anderson. He explained the treaties and his support for the President, answered questions and informed us that the Vice-President had invited us for coffee prior to the briefing, which was scheduled for 2:00 p.m. Once more we got into the cars. This time we were driven to the White House.

The White House

I do not know how many of you have ever been to the White House, but I had never been inside it before. Perhaps it was naivete, perhaps provincialism, but I felt my skin rising — I felt a sense of history — as we rode up to the black iron gate in our black limousine and I gave my driver's license to the guard for inspection and identification. Soon we were at the portico of the North Entrance and into the Roosevelt Room.

It is called the Roosevelt Room because there are portraits of Teddy and Franklin Roosevelt on the walls. We stood sipping our coffee, admiring the room, when suddenly one of the doors opened and in walked the Vice President, with the President close behind. There was an immediate silence — even a hush — and one of the great thrills I have known was to be introduced to the

President of the United States by the Vice President there in the White House.

I shall not detail for you the briefing to the eighty or so representatives from Minnesota, Pennsylvania and Virginia, except to tell you that we met with officials of the State and Defense Departments, the Joint Chiefs and the President. At 5:00 p.m. the briefing was over and at 7:30 we were back in Minneapolis.

And I must tell you that in the days that followed, and as I thought of my experience, the essential feeling I had was one of gratitude — not merely to the President, the Vice President and to Senator Anderson, but of all things to my grandparents. More than three-quarters of a century ago, each set, one independent of the other, made that perilous and harrowing trip from Eastern Europe to Boston, Massachusetts. And now their grandson had been to the White House with the President.

They had a vision — those grandparents of mine — an intuitive sense of what this country was — or could be: the land of the free; the land where a man's worth was in his ability, not his religion or race; a land where one could rise to any height. They had a vision. How do I show them my gratitude? How do I repay them for their daring, their hope, their dreams? There is only one way — only one way — and that is simply this: I must do all I can to keep this land — to make it the "goldene medina," the promised land, they envisioned.

And I say to you, each one of us has an ancestor — most everyone here has ancestors who made a similar voyage, who had a similar desire, a similar reaching out, a similar dream and hope. Let's be grateful for them this Thanksgiving Day — and pledge to show them our gratitude.

President Sadat

I have just returned — late yesterday — from San Francsicso, where I attended for five days a series of meetings called "Judaism in a Secular Age." Some 4,000 people were present. I do not know how President Sadat's visit to Israel affected you here, but for us, it was a highly charged, deeply emotional time.

On Sunday morning, we overcrowded the huge ballroom at the Fairmount Hotel to see on closed circuit television a hastily compiled documentary of all the events that had taken place in the Middle East and we were thankful. Some wept tears of thanksgiving.

We were thankful that President Sadat would go, not merely to Israel, but to Jerusalem, where the United States does not have an embassy. It was a complete recognition of the land. We were thankful for his bravery, his fortitude, his desire for peace. We were thankful for the young lives his action may well have spared.

And I want to repeat for you the words of His Excellency Simcha Dinitz, the Israeli Ambassador to the United States, who spoke to us soon thereafter. "I must tell you," he said, "the Middle East will now never be the same. President Sadat and Prime Minister Begin were both satisfied with their conversations. Never before have I had the hopes for peace that I now have."

There was a demonstration of Arab students outside our convention headquarters that day. They carried signs reading "Death to Sadat," "Sadat is a traitor," "Sadat is a murderous Zionist." "If this is what takes place in San Francisco," I said to myself, "what must it be like in Syria or Libya or wherever the P.L.O. exists?"

I have thought much about the events of that weekend and I am not only thankful to Mr. Sadat, I am grateful — not merely for his initiative, and all that it may mean, but there is something else. Because of him we have been taught once again what one single human being can do. What he did was on an international scale, but you and I are aware that there is so much hostility, so much rancor, so much anger among people you and I know, among our contemporaries, our peers, in our families, among those dear to us. Isn't now, once again, a time for reaching out, for harmony, for fresh starts. Isn't now the time to be just a bit kinder, just a whit more concerned, just a little more loving than we have ever been. Isn't that the way to show our gratitude, this Thanksgiving Day, for what happened half a world away, but also to us.

Dr. Yaacov Yankelevich

One more personal reference.

Dr. Yaacov Yankelevich is a Russian Jew. He was head of the Department of Obstetrics at the leading hospital in Kiev and a full professor at the medical school there. His father had held the same posts before him. But Russia was restrictive for him and his family. Even he — despite the position he held — felt the stings of anti-Semitism. And he decided to try to leave.

When Dr. Yankelevich announced his intention, he was stripped of his job. His son was dropped from school, his wife was forced to leave work. But they prevailed and two years ago they arrived in Minneapolis.

Put yourself in his place. Fifty-two years old. Hardly able to speak English, unable to understand the special language and shorthand of your professional colleagues. Examinations to be taken, examinations in basic science that most doctors do not use and have forgotten. Somehow Dr. Yankelevich found himself a job as a scrub nurse in one of our hospitals — a work demeaning, I suspect, for one who had been an outstanding surgeon in similar operating rooms.

I do not know how Dr. Yankelevich came to me — but he came with a request — "Help me," he said, "help me to be retrained. I am willing to study. I am willing to go to school. I am willing to do anything. Help me."

Last June Dr. Yankelevich passed all of his examinations. He is now an intern — six months at Mt. Sinai Hospital, six months at the University hospitals. And then he shall begin again. "You have saved my life," he said to me recently.

And I have thought much about Dr. Yankelevich these past weeks — and I am grateful to him, even more than he is grateful to me. I am grateful not merely for the divine gifts of spirit and determination, not merely for the human ability to overcome trauma and tribulation. I am grateful to him that he gave me the opportunity to help!

The Opportunity To Help

And there are so many opportunities for us to help. But you and I know that often we have eyes, but we do not see; we have ears, but we do not hear; we have hearts, but we do not feel.

But we were made in God's image, you and I. Thank God for that! We can renew ourselves, we can be sensitized to His word, to our respective traditions, we can do His will. We may not be able to love our neighbors as ourselves — that may be a psychological impossibility — but we can be aware of their needs, their feelings. If there is any means for us to be grateful this Thanksgiving Day — to somehow repay for the goodness that we have known — that just has to be the way.

And so we pray:

Heavenly Father — We are humbly grateful for all that is ours: our families, our friends and our dear ones; for this blessed land in which we live. And we pray that You will grant us the desire, the will, the purpose and the fortitude so to live that others will be grateful for us — that somehow our lives have touched theirs in goodness.

Amen

Where Do We Turn?
The Challenge to the Synagogue

October 8 (Rosh Hashanah), 1973

One of my major concerns, and also a major theme of my sermons, has been the primacy of the synagogue in American Jewish life.

In an age of secularization and a time when many American Jews have found their Jewish expression in community centers, defense agencies, in the host of Jewish organizations and especially in a commitment to Israel, the place of the synagogue as the bedrock of Jewish life has often been overlooked or shunted aside.

The Watergate episode presented an opportunity to put the "primacy" that means so much to me in perspective. I attempted to do so on Rosh Hashanah, 1973. It was a time when former President Nixon was fighting for his political life. As you know, he became the first president to resign from office almost a year later, August 24, 1974.

* * * *

There are many thoughts that come to my mind as I stand here this evening, many thoughts and many feelings. Once again it is time for Jews to add another digit to the calendar. The year 5733 with all that it has brought us — its joys and its sorrows, its disappointments, frustrations, its successes, is now history.

Once again it is time to greet one another, to express our love to one another — our hopes for one another. It is time to clasp the extended hand, to say "L'shanah Tovah" and to pray that the year to come will bring us good health and continued purpose; contentment and peace.

Once again it is Rosh Hashanah, a time to slow our every day pace just a bit, a time to stop for a moment — a time to look anew at ourselves and our direction. It is a time for evaluation — not casually or superficially, not as mere dinner table talk, but openly, honestly — searchingly. It is time to measure the distance between our values and our conduct.

Another year has gone. 365 precious days. Did they bring us goodness, rejoicing, affection? Another year has gone. Did our loves deepen? Were our hopes attained? A year of our lives has sped by. Dear ones who were with us just a few moments ago are no longer at our side. A home that was so loving, it seemed, is broken. Children are no longer children. Youngsters are suddenly grown up and away. School has begun again. Will there be new friends? What shall we accomplish?

It is Rosh Hashanah. Whatever else we may have done with our days and the year now ended, it is time, now, to take a few moments — if only these few moments — to move away from the rush and routine of every day, to take account of what the past year has brought us, to try to understand who we have become and where we are heading.

Watergate

I must tell you that I had not intended to speak about Watergate this evening. Seemingly there is no need. You have read the articles I have read. You have seen the faces, you have heard the voices I have seen and heard. You have been shocked, amazed, disgusted, confused, and titillated just as I have been. But the more I thought about this day and its meaning, this day of introspection and soul searching, the more I knew that for me to stand in this place dedicated to God, consecrated to the teachings of our faith — and not to mention Watergate — would be a form of blasphemy! For me, your Rabbi, to stand here on this day, a day insisting that we examine our collective souls, and to close my eyes to such an affront to the moral values of our society; for me to be silent when such a blatant insensitivity to corruption has touched us all, would be a desecration! It would be a disservice to our faith, to this day, and to you.

And I do not ask about who laundered what money, who made what lists, who covered up for whom. I do not ask about the new legislation that may emerge, or the after effects, on our political system. I do not even ask the question Senator Baker so persistently asked: "Why?" or "How could this have happened to us?" It is not answers to all these I search for this evening, important as they may be. There is something even more compelling that I want to know, something I believe we must know.

The Question I Ask

This is a great and wonderful land in which we live. It is a land we love — a land that has meant so much to our fathers and to us. It was their dream come true — and ours too. And now we

71

see a cynicism and crassness, a distrust and a dishonestly, a discrediting of moral leadership never before revealed to us in such starkness. We see exposed in the highest places of our government a mentality, that given its way, would rob us of the kind of life our fathers sought and for which so many of us fought.

And the question I ask is a simple but, I believe, a pertinent one. Where do we turn to blunt the trend? To whom do we turn to stop the contagion? Who — what will recapture for us all that we always thought we were? Who will point up for us consistently and without fear, the folly of instant gratification, the evil of greedy materialism, the curse of winning at any price? Where do we go from here? Or do we simply say "leave it to the courts", "punish the culprits" — and then make of Watergate just a passing phase, another form of entertainment, a conversation piece, an experience we hasten to forget?

Where Do We Turn

Do we turn to the Government for moral guidance? We have seen lying become commonplace, records falsified, influence sold, peaceful countries invaded and despoiled — we have seen dictators supported, despots assisted. And this has not been limited to one time, one place, one political party. Convenience, compromise, expediency, sheer power are too often the necessary tools of government. Who of you would count on it to make us moral?

Do we turn to the business community? Do we ask Standard Oil of California to set our standard? Shall it be to G.E. we look? Or The American Tobacco Co.? Will it be Bethlehem Steel or Honeywell or I.T.T.? I know and you know that advancement in corporate life comes not from moral concern but from fiscal creativity!

Of course there are men and corporations increasingly concerned with social welfare and ethical matters. Thank God for that. But you and I also know that that is not the general concern of business. Who of you would turn to the business community for your moral guide?

Do we turn to the Educational Institutions? Do they have the answer? Some of the men who paraded before our television sets, answering questions from the Senate Watergate Committee, were products of the best schooling this country has to offer. Last year's University of Oklahoma's football team had to forfeit 8 wins and a Sugar Bowl Victory because an assistant coach falsified the academic transcript of two freshmen stars. College professors are alleged to be spending more time as consultants than they are as teachers. Yet they know we send our children to learn from them, and it is for this that they serve on faculties. A youngster wins a Soapbox Derby by fraud. Students seek grades and recommendations often by any means. Shoplifting has become almost a national sport for some kids. Housewives and employees have joined the game. And every one of them has been to school.

Should we then turn to the press? Will the newspapers be the source of our standards? Or should it be the weeklies? *Time Magazine* perhaps, or *Newsweek*? Will it be the Hearst Press or the *New York Times,* the Cowles Publications or the *Chicago Tribune*? Shall they be the assessor of our morals?

Or will we turn to the scientists? Is theirs the discipline that disseminates and perpetuates ethics in our society? Morality, as you know, is incidental to pure science. Science does not seek to make moral decisions. It does not want to. The judgement of what is right and what is wrong stands outside the scientific domain.

Our Secular Society

Left to itself, a secular society, no matter how exalted its principles, will in time succumb to the pressures of vested interests. The guardian of the young man who cheated in the Soapbox Derby shrugged it off by saying, "Everyone has been doing it for years." The excusers of Watergate tell us, "Everyone has been doing it for years." A Louis Harris Survey shows that 69% of us, among whom are so many who shudder at the "White House Horrors," say the same thing: "Everyone has been doing it for years." The rule of thumb becomes, "Do what you can get away with." The most common advice becomes, "Don't get caught."

So where do we go? We know something is wrong. We know something is very wrong. What do we do?

Should we turn to the family. Where better can love be taught, goodness extolled, righteous living displayed. Can we turn to the family which in Jewish life has always been a "small sanctuary?" Can we turn to it? But the family is not vocal. It does not extend beyond its own confines. It does not point the accusing finger at society, and examples within it are not necessarily exemplary. It can be a source for bigotry and cruelty and intolerance. And tragically, the family is currently in disarray and in jeopardy.

The only institution in our society primarily concerned with morality, principally devoted to the teaching of justice, love and compassion, is the religious institution. And for us that means Judaism and this Temple. The only voice in your life that consistently cries out "Stop. You must not use another human being. You must not degrade, debase or destroy him," is your Jewish faith. The only stricture upon you that constantly commands, "Stop this self-indulgence. Stop this concern only with self. You have an obligation to your family. Pursue justice, proclaim liberty. Love your neighbor. You shall not commit adultery," comes from your Judaism.

Where else will you find it. Where else? From television? The movies? Where else can you find this from among all the influences that touch us? From where will your children learn it? It undergirds the family; it strengthens the family. It supports and substantiates it. And it proclaims these truths over and over again. Often your ears are deaf. Often you do not like what it says. Often its voice is not strong enough. But it is never stilled. Never.

A True Religion

I cannot give you all the answers to what infects our society and our lives, but I do know this. Without a moral transcendence, without a law higher than the ones we ourselves make, the standards set by society are shaky. Without a belief in God, ethical persistency becomes a futile hope.

I cannot tell what other religious groups should do, but I do know this. A Judaism that tells you only what you want to hear, a Judaism that does not prod your conscience and disturb you, a Judaism that does not goad you to ethical living, is not authentic Judaism. It is a snare and a delusion.

I also know this. A religion true to itself and to you cannot be divorced from politics. A Judaism completely divorced from politics is a Judaism divorced from life, for the decisions politicians make often determine how we shall live, and far too often, who of us shall die.

And one thing more. In our long history we Jews were never totally adjusted to society. We have been part of it, and yet we have been apart from it. Perhaps God favored us with that role.

Abraham would not adjust to idolatry. Moses would not adjust to slavery. Our prophets would not adjust to the tyranny, the evil, the debauchery and the wars of their day. And we who are their heirs must not adjust now. You and I must never be lulled into indifference by affluence, acculturation or acceptance. We must never become unconcerned with wrong, inured to corruption, apathetic to the immorality around us.

And for this we need a Judaism that is vital and forthright. We need a Temple that is strong and has your concern. We need a Judaism that our kids find believable. No other Jewish institution has the mission that is ours. You and your family can play tennis and paddle ball at the J.C.C. You can swim in an Olympic-sized swimming pool, you can study Hebrew, support Hadassah, the Council of Jewish Women, Mt. Sinai Hospital or Brandeis. You may give generously to the Federation and buy Israel bonds. The B'nai B'rith or ORT may be your thing. But Jewish life, Jewish living, the ethical structure of your being stems from the Synagogue. If you want your children and grandchildren to learn this, if you want these other institutions to continue, then we at Temple must have the needed environment, the needed tools to teach it! For this we need your support when we call upon you. And we shall call upon you. For we must. We cannot do it otherwise.

Our 95th Year

This is the 95th year of our Temple. In every generation it was challenged to greatness and to primacy. The challenge in our day is more difficult, more perplexing, more complicated than ever before. The times we live in, the influences upon us — the mores of our age, confront us and our tradition. They dare us to hold firm to the values that have been ours.

And we must accept the challenge. I cannot accept it for you. You cannot accept it for me. We must do this together! We must grasp the opportunity that is ours, the opportunity to build on the magnificent foundation given us; so that we, too, as were those in their generation, may be remembered for blessing.

Each day as I enter the Temple, I say a silent prayer. I thank God that there are men and women in this Congregation who care — men and women of high motive; men and women of serious purpose and great determination; men and women who are earnestly concerned with the Temple and its future — for the future of Jewish life in this community depends upon you and them.

I thank God for them as I ask God's blessing upon us now.

Our God and Father, be with us as we begin the New Year and the tasks ahead. We need your guidance. We need your help.

Whatever is good in us, strengthen and bless. Whatever ideals we cherish, help us to see them more clearly. Whatever high purposes we set before us, help us to pursue them more resolutely. Whatever loves and dear ones we have, help us to love them more fully. And may we so live and so provide that our beloved congregation may continue to be strengthened so that our faith may flourish and Jewish life prosper.

May it be so, O Lord.

Amen

NOBLE PRIZES

Almost every year, since 1963, at a time when the Nobel Prizes were being awarded in Stockholm, I would give a sermon called "Noble Prizes," The opening paragraphs have always been the same — except for the monetary amount received by the prize winners. That has changed. And the concluding paragraph has always been the same. In between I have given "Noble Prizes" to men and women, some obscure, some famous, who at the risk to their own lives, safety and careers, or at the risk to the lives and well being of their families, have nonetheless courageously given of themselves to what was right and good.

Most of the names are unknown to you. There is for example Daniel O'Brien, a schoolteacher in Kettering, Ohio, who lost his job because he refused to give in to the pressures of the Right Wing in his town. There is Sylvia Zalmanson and Boris Kochubyevsky, Russian dissidents jailed for their devotion to freedom. There is Dr. James Silver, Professor of History at the University of Mississippi, for his struggle against prejudice, and Albert Sachs who was cast out of South Africa for the same reason and many others.

Here is "Noble Prizes, 1976" which was given on February 4, 1977, plus a few of the others whom I have chosen over the years.

* * * *

Noble Prizes, 1976
February 4, 1977

In 1896, a Swedish chemist and industrialist named Alfred Bernhard Nobel died. Nobel had invented dynamite and because of this became one of the world's wealthiest men. But he was a troubled man, haunted by the fact that he had created something which could be — and was — used for so much death and destruction. In his will, he therefore provided a fund of $9,000,000, the interest of which was to be awarded to individuals who had made valuable contributions to humanity in five fields — chemistry, physics, physiology or medicine, literature, and international peace.

Since 1901, when the first grants were made, there have been some 400 Nobel prizes. Recipients do not apply for the awards, the average value of which is approximately $122,000, and more than one individual can share in each grant. Rather, they are selected by various committees from Sweden. For example, the medical faculty at the University of Stockholm picks the winner of the award for medicine; and a committee of five, elected by the Swedish Parliament, selects the winner for peace. Announcements of recipients are made at different times of the year, and occasionally, when no one is found worthy of a grant, no award is made in that particular field.

This evening, as I have done so often in the past, I should like to make some awards of my own, three to be exact. They are not Nobel Prizes and carry no cash award. They are Noble Prizes and carry only my gratitude, respect and admiration. They are not for excellence in the sciences, or literature or the pursuit of peace. They are for excellence in concern, in thoughtfulness and in the promise that humanity holds.

Noble Prize #1 — to **Yefim Davidovich;** *Colonel, Army of the Union of Soviet Socialist Republics; Minsk, Russia. Deceased April 26, 1976. For devotion to human rights.*

Yefim Davidovich was 54 years old when he died. He was a Jew. In his younger years he was trained as a professional soldier and fought in all the fury of World War II. He was wounded four times, and received numerous medals and military citations for his bravery and ability. When the war was over, he was a colonel and commanded what was considered to be a model regiment. He was designated as a "Hero of the Red Army," an accolade not given to many.

In 1969 Colonel Davidovich suffered a heart attack. While recuperating, he passed the time reading books from a local library, jotting down in the margins his personal views on Russian personalities, including Stalin. At this time also, provoked by the unrestrained anti-Semitic outpourings in the Soviet press, he took to writing letters to Russian agencies and officials.

Somehow the books he had read during his illness got into the hands of Russian authorities, and two years later, in 1971, it was determined that Davidovich was the author of the marginal notes. Because of this and his letters, there now began a harrassment and persecution by the KGB that contributed to — and only ended with — his death.

His house was searched and copies of the letters were confiscated. A gun, a war souvenir that he had kept, was also found. He was charged with spreading anti-Soviet propaganda, with possessing weapons illegally, and taken to jail. Another heart attack followed. "My only crime," Davidovich explained, "is my feeling of elementary human dignity against lies and slander."

Because it was the period when Leonid Brezhnev was to visit the United States and the Russian authorities feared a world reaction if Davidovich was brought to trial, he was released with warnings and an order not to leave Minsk.

Now he understood better than ever before the official Russian attitude toward Jews. But despite the danger to himself and his family, he would not be silenced.

In May, 1976, in full military uniform, Colonel Davidovich spoke at a memorial service commemorating the Jews of Minsk killed during World War II. In the presence of hundreds of Jews, he described the misery of the Minsk ghetto and the final solution of the Nazis. He spoke of the liquidation of Jewish culture under Stalin and the murder of Yiddish writers. He lashed out against the suppression of Jewish cultural and religious facilities in the U.S.S.R.

Well, you can imagine what happened. Colonel Davidovich was arrested, stripped of his rank and military pension, and confined to his home. Again his heart failed. Again he recovered.

Now Jews from all over the world began a move to get him out of the country. An appeal was made to Soviet officialdom to allow Davidovich and his family to emigrate. Nothing resulted. He petitioned over and over again. Every request was denied. Agitated and distressed, his weakened heart unable to stand the constant pressure, Colonel Davidovich suffered a third heart attack last April. He was denied permission to enter a hospital and died at home.

"What the Hitlerites had been unable to do," wrote 32 Soviet Jewish activists after his death, "has been cold-bloodedly done by the butchers of the KGB. He was murdered through psychological terror, threats, blackmail and provocations, cruelly and senselessly."

Colonel Davidovich is dead — but his words, his actions, his life these past years are an inspiration to all those still beleagured in the U.S.S.R.

Noble Prize #1 — to Yefim Davidovich; Colonel, Army of the

Soviet Socialist Republics; Minsk, Russia. Deceased. For devotion to human rights.

* * * *

Noble Prize #2 — To Betty Williams; *Housewife; Belfast, Ireland. For devotion to peace and human life.*

On August 10, Betty Williams, age 33, was driving home from her invalid mother's house in the Catholic district of Belfast, when she saw an IRA driver shot through the heart by a British soldier. The car he was in spun out of control, hitting a woman pedestrian and her three children. The woman was rushed to intensive care at the Royal Victorian Hospital. The three children — Joanne 8, John 3, and Andrew 6 weeks — were dead.

Betty Williams, sickened by the sight, decided that she would no longer sit out the bloodshed. She had had enough Catholic killing Protestant, Protestant killing Catholic, British soldiers killing and dying. The next day, with a sister and a friend, note pads in hand, she set off into the IRA part of town. She knocked on doors. She talked. She got signatures. Within hours she had hundreds of names on a peace petition.

The next day, 200 women marched in the streets with her. On their way, they passed the home of the aunt of the dead children. She, too, joined the demonstration and became a leader with Betty Williams. Within a week, there was a second march. This time there were 10,000 women from both sides of the conflict. Many of them pushed baby carriages. Some walked with little children. The following Saturday there was a third march. Now 20,000 women streamed into the rally from the Protestant and Catholic districts. They carried makeshift banners bearing the names of their streets and demanding peace.

Betty Williams has not received universal acclaim for her call to life. "Death to Betty Williams," reads a slogan scrawled on a roadway near her home. She has been threatened. Her home has been fired. She has received obscene letters. She has had to send her own children away to safety. But she won't be deterred.

"I am scared out of my wits," she says, "but we will not be intimidated by these things any more."

Peace has not come to Northern Ireland. Bombs still explode. Deaths do occur. But the marches go on. Tens of thousands come together every week. Financial support is growing. And there is hope. If the killing is to stop, it will be because of the spirit, the bravery, the will of the likes of Betty Williams.

Noble Prize #2 — to Betty Williams; Housewife; Belfast, Ireland. For devotion to peace and human life.

* * * *

Noble Prize #3 — To Michal Bacos; *Pilot, Air France Flight #139; Paris, France. For devotion to human decency. For bravery beyond duty.*

I know very little about Michal Bacos. Almost nothing has been written about him. All I know is that he is 52 years old, he has a wife and two children, and that he was the captain of the French aircraft that was hijacked last June 27 and flown to Entebbe, Uganda.

Most of us can repeat the story of those harrowing days and the exciting, inspiring, miraculous rescue. But most of our conversation, our thoughts, our memories, as the months pass, will be on the daring decisions, the daring flight, the daring attack, the meticulous preparation, the joyous return. We will not talk much about Michal Bacos.

But do you remember what took place between the crime and the rescue? The flight, hijacked out of Athens, made a stop at Benghazi in Libya for refueling. There was a woman passenger who was pregnant and sick, and was allowed to leave the plane.

Six and a half hours later, at 11:00 p.m., exactly twelve hours after having left Athens, the flight took off again. This time for its final destination. The next day, Monday, June 28, the startling events began to unfold. Big Daddy President Amin appeared in obvious cooperation with the terrorists, but portrayed himself as the peaceful negotiator. Israel was informed that unless the hijackers' demands were met, the hostages would be murdered.

The world, however, did not know what was taking place in the old terminal building at Entebbe, where the hostages were being held. First there was a "selection" process, reminiscent of the concentration camps. Jews were separated from the other passengers. And then came the sudden freeing of the 47 passengers who were not Jewish, an event even more reminiscent of Nazi barbarism. "First, separate the Jews from the others. Then let the world know they are expendable!" Who would complain? Who would speak out? Who would come to their rescue? No one did in the 1940's. Would anyone in 1976?

One voice was heard. We did not hear it, far removed as we were. But the hijackers did. Only Michal Bacos spoke up. Only he demanded what was right. He could have been freed. He and his crew could have boarded that plane for Paris. He could have gone home to his wife and children. No one would fault him. No one would call him coward, traitor, villain. But he refused to go. He demanded to stay with his passengers. He ordered his crew to do the same. He had no idea what would happen. He could not be sure what the terrorists or Idi Amin would do. Suppose the deadline had not been met? Suppose the passengers were systematically put to death? There was no guarantee that he would leave alive.

The rescue is now history. In the book *90 Minutes at Entebbe* there is a picture of the hostages emerging safely from the giant planes on Israeli soil. Michal Bacos is among them. And his smile and beaming face reflect the same joy and relief as those of all his freed passengers.

Noble Prize #3 — to Michal Bacos; Pilot, Air France Flight #139; Paris, France. For devotion to human decency. For bravery beyond duty.

* * * *

Nobel prizes are won by few. It takes skill, training, opportunity, perseverance and sometimes luck. Noble prizes can be won by all. It just takes being human. It just takes fulfilling one of God's purposes for us here on earth. Try it.

* * * *

From "Noble Prizes," 1956

Noble Prize #1 — To Hazel Brannon Smith; *Editor, "The Lexington Advertiser," Lexington, Mississippi. For devotion to human decency.*

Hazel Smith was born in Gadsden, Alabama, fifty-one years ago. Her father was an electrical contractor. She was brought up by a Negro nurse.

At the University of Alabama, where she went to school, her interest centered on journalism, and when she was graduated in

1935, she hunted for a country newspaper sick enough to buy and well enough to nurse back to health. She found such a paper in the town of Durant, Mississippi, a paper that had 600 subscribers, a paper from which three editors had run in thirteen months.

In four years the Durant *News* was paid for. In a few more years, Mrs. Smith was able to purchase the much bigger Lexington *Advertiser* whose subscriptions were sold all over the county, and a short time later, she acquired two more local weeklies.

Almost in two decades, from 1935-54, Hazel Smith built a debt-free profitable business and earned a tremendous amount of "good will" with the people of her community. Living was good for her and her husband. They had a lovely home. They had purchased a farm. She wore Hattie Carnegie hats. She traded in her Cadillac convertible every year or so.

But then in 1954 things changed. The Supreme Court outlawed segregated schools. Violence against Negroes became the order of the day in Mississippi. And when Hazel Smith attacked that violence in her press, when she pleaded for the rights and liberties of the Negro population, racists laid siege to her, her life was endangered, rumors were spread about her, anonymous hate sheets were distributed, libel suits were filed against her, and a competing weekly was established to run her out of business. In succeeding weeks vandals surrounded her house and tore up $300 worth of lawn furniture; a cross was burned at her front door; one of her newspaper offices was bombed. On succeeding days, delegations of white citizens systematically called upon all retailers who ran ads in her paper, urging them to stop. Only one local merchant held out as did the manufacturing plant in Lexington and the statewide Mississippi Power and Light Company.

Soon Hazel Smith was over her head in red ink. $100,000 worth. No one believed her papers would survive. But she kept on. She mortgaged the property she owned — the newspaper buildings, the farm and her home. Her work force of 15 full timers shrank to 5. She bought a down-payment Rambler. She just would not succumb.

Hazel Smith is still in business. In 1964 her editorials won a Pulitzer Prize. Last year the Columbia University Journalism Review announced the Hazel Brannon Smith Fund to assure her continued publication. Yet all this has not been the answer for her. One of my friends spoke to her last week and told me she is still in great financial difficulty — still struggling desperately. But her papers, thank Heavens, continue to decry racism, violence and tyranny.

Noble Prize #1 — to Hazel Brannon Smith; Editor, *The Lexington Advertiser*, Lexington, Mississippi. For devotion to human decency.

* * * *

From "Noble Prizes," 1966

My first award this year is to **Dr. Samuel Belkin;** *Rabbi; President of Yeshiva University, New York City, N.Y. And the award: for devotion to the Jewish people.*

Yeshiva University is an institution unique in the world. Besides being a university in our western sense, it contains the largest and most influential Orthodox Rabbinic Seminary in the United States, and perhaps in existence. Its faculty is a noted one; its graduates are in virtually every community of this country; and its influence in Jewish life is great and will undoubtedly increase.

The Synagogue Council of America is also an organization unique in the world. It is the only one in existence whose membership is limited to the three great branches of American Jewish religious life. It looks upon itself and is generally recognized as the official spokesman of the total Jewish religious community in America. The Council is the meeting place where Reform, Orthodox and Conservative Jewish leaders can come together, can discuss issues of common concern, and can authentically express a common Jewish religious point of view.

On November 6, the Synagogue Council of America held its 40th Anniversary Dinner. The event of the evening was to be the presentation of awards to the three distinguished presidents of the three great Jewish Seminaries in America: Dr. Nelson Glueck of the Hebrew Union College; Dr. Louis Finkelstein of the Jewish Theological Seminary; and Dr. Samuel Belkin of Yeshiva University.

All three men accepted the invitation to receive the honor; but when it became public, there was a shrill and immediate protest from the so-called "right wing" Orthodox rabbis of the country. They demanded that Dr. Belkin retract his acceptance. They insisted that his appearance at the same dinner and on the same platform with Dr. Glueck and Dr. Finkelstein would be tacit approval of those two men and the branches of Judaism they represent. "We publicly disassociate ourselves from the indirect endorsement of the Conservative and Reform movements," they declared in a large advertisement which appeared in the *New York Times.* "We direct the attention of the Jewish community to our total negation of these dangerous and alien ideologies which threaten the very fabric of Torah Judaism and Jewish life."

Dr. Belkin was faced with a choice: Is Orthodoxy the only Judaism there can be? Is Reform alien? Is Conservative Judaism dangerous? Is it more important that the Orthodox elements of American Judaism be united than to admit that Conservative and Reform Judaism have a place in Jewish life? Over and over again pressures had been exerted in the meetings of the Union of American Orthodox Congregations for official Orthodox Jewry to withdraw from the Synagogue Council of America. Year after year such resolutions had been defeated. But that had been an internal struggle. Now the issue was public. And Dr. Belkin was faced with the dilemma.

To me and to you, perhaps, the decision would have been a simple one. But students of Yeshiva University were threatening to picket the meeting of the Synagogue Council. A bomb threat was received by Dr. Belkin. Leading Orthodox rabbis and laymen who opposed the Council made their opinions known and their voices heard. And Dr. Belkin was not just a rabbi whose acts were binding upon himself and a congregation. He would be committing Yeshiva University to an ideology. He would be affirming a point of view that would be taught to future generations of Orthodox rabbis. He was placing his position as President of Yeshiva University in jeopardy. He would be defying so-called "Torah Judaism." He would be acting contrary to the wishes of many of his own alumni and Board.

Dr. Belkin appeared at the meeting of the Synagogue Council. Dr. Belkin walked through the pickets from the school and from other Yeshivas. He repudiated right wing orthodoxy. He sat with the presidents of the other Jewish Seminaries. He received recognition along with them. Whatever the future of his own place in Orthodox Jewish life might be, whatever the criticism he might henceforth receive, he chose to help solidify and unify the American Jewish community.

Noble Prize #1 — to Dr. Samuel Belkin; rabbi; President of Yeshiva University, New York City, N.Y. For devotion to Judaism.

* * * *

From "Noble Prizes," 1966

Noble Prize #3 — To Charles Longstreet Weltner; *Congressman; House of Representatives, Washington, D.C. For devotion to America.*

Charles Longstreet Weltner is 39 years old. He is a handsome man, an attorney, a descendant of a distinguished Southern family. His grandfather wrote the Confederate Constitution and was killed at Fredericksberg during the Civil War. His father was a university president. In 1962 Charles Weltner was elected to the House of Representatives from Atlanta, Georgia. He was reelected in 1964.

Congressman Weltner was unusual among Southern representatives. In his first major congressional address, he indicted Southern leaders who were silent at the southern treatment of the Negro and the violence in southern streets. He became the first Representative from the deep South to have a Negro on his staff. He was the only Southerner to vote for the Civil Rights Bills. And it was he who initiated the Congressional investigation of the Ku Klux Klan.

In the fall of this year Mr. Weltner had to run again for office. He was overwhelmingly endorsed in the Democratic primary which is tantamount to election in his state. As part of the procedure of the Democratic Party in Georgia, every endorsed candidate must sign a pledge to support all the party nominees in the general election. This Charles Weltner did.

No one expected, no one dreamed — least of all Congressman Weltner — that Lester Maddox would be the Democratic nominee for Governor of the State of Georgia. And I need not tell you that Mr. Maddox, former restauranteur, is one of the most rabid segregationists in the South. He is the man who used guns and axe handles to drive Negroes away from his cafeteria, and the picture appeared in every paper in the country. He is a man who campaigned with segregation as the basis for his political program.

Now Weltner faced a choice. His record in Congress had been outstanding. His future in politics was most bright. He had been spoken of often as a future governor or a United States Senator. And he had taken an oath to support the Democratic candidate, who now was Lester Maddox, a man whose political philosophy he could not abide.

A few days after the Primary, Congressman Weltner held a news conference in his office. He read a statement to the reporters.

"Today," he said, "the one man in our State who exists as the very symbol of violence and oppression is the Democratic nominee for the highest office in Georgia. His entire public career is directly contrary to my deepest convictions and beliefs. And while I cannot violate my oath neither can I violate my principles. I would rather give up my office. Therefore I am withdrawing as the Democratic nominee for the House of Representatives."

Charles Weltner's career as a public figure may have been completely destroyed. His hopes for higher office have undoubtedly been demolished. His future in government may be no more. But he preferred his integrity. He elected his vision of an America that is free and democratic rather than elective office and his own undisturbed advancement.

Noble Prize #3 — to Charles Longstreet Weltner; Congressman; House of Representatives, Washington, D.C. For devotion to America.

*   *   *   *

From "Noble Prizes," 1969

My first award is a posthumous award. It goes to **Dr. Janusz Korczak;** *physician; Warsaw, Poland. For devotion to decency.*

Janusz Korczak was born in Warsaw in 1878. He received his medical degree in that city in 1905 and took advanced training in pediatrics in Berlin and Paris. He then returned to Warsaw to head the pediatric department of an important hospital for children, pioneering in child psychology.

In 1915 he gave up his medical practice and became administrator of a Jewish orphanage to devote his entire time to educational reform. He wrote numerous children's books — books which were translated into several languages and enjoyed great popularity. But his main thrust in life was as an educator and theoretician in the field of social pedagogy. As such he is counted among the great pioneers: Pestolazzi, Montessori, Froebe, and Dewey.

Under his direction the orphanage became known as the "Home of the Child," and the "Free Children's Republic." His teachers and aides were vigorously indoctrinated with the concept of "abundance of love" for their wards, and were trained to create an environment of humaneness, security and affection. His educational philosophy was simple. He demanded respect for the child, and the right to its own individuality and independence. He opposed the use of force under any circumstance. He organized the children into a society based on principles of brotherhood, equal rights and obligations, and justice. They were taught to carry on all activities, set the rules, conduct a children's court, and participate in the functions of the adult board of directors. How foresighted he was. Proudly, Dr. Korczak saw his children flourish and mature with personalities neither warped nor embittered by orphanage rearing.

Then came the Nazis — and the Warsaw ghetto. 400,000 children were constricted in that dismal area, and Dr. Korczak wanted to protect them all.

He pleaded with everyone in the ghetto for funds to provide food and care for the children and the people gave of their meager means. But it could not be enough and there was always less and less to eat. Then the order came from the Nazis. The children of the orphan homes were to be sent to Auschwitz and the crematorium. Doctor Korczak could have saved himself. He was not wanted. His name was not on the list. How long he could have been spared, no one knows. But the opportunity was there.

This man would not abandon his children. On August 12, 1942, a long line of children formed in front of the orphanage, some with school books under their arms. It was a procession of small, emaciated, weak, shriveled, shrunken children. But no one was crying. For Dr. Korczak was at the head of the line. Listen to an eyewitness account of what took place:

> Hitler's child-killers were seized by a mad frenzy and began firing their guns. The children did not utter a cry, none made an attempt to run away, none sought to hide. They looked up at their teacher and protector, their father and brother, Dr. Janusz Korczak. He stood in front to protect his children with his emaciated body. The Nazis showed no mercy. A pistol in one hand, a whip in the other — they shouted and ordered the children to march to the death trains. Dr. Korczak, hatless, held the youngest child by the hand and marched out front. Behind him marched the nurses and the children to their slaughter. The very cobblestones wept.

Dr. Korczak went to his death. The nobility of his act, in a world racked with violence and hate, we cannot let die.

Noble Prize #1 — To Janusz Korczak, Physician, Educator, Social Worker, Idealist. For devotion to decency.

ON MARRIAGE AND FAMILY

One of my prime interests in the Rabbinate has been marriage and family counseling.

My interest began when I was a student at the Hebrew Union College and was simultaneously studying at the University of Cincinnati for a Doctorate in Education. I took a course in counseling at the University and discovered that it was more than merely "talking and listening" or even offering advice, but that there were diverse theories and concepts; and that there could be careful diagnostic and calculated approaches to the problems that families face. And more than that, there was also the prospect of solving them.

As I began to do the counseling that is part of every rabbi's day, I realized very soon how little I really knew. To compensate, I took to reading extensively in the field; I took courses at the University of Minnesota; I spent three months in the Department of Family Relations at Florida State University in Tallahassee in a special doctoral program; and I worked at a Marriage and Family Counseling Clinic in Minneapolis — all to sharpen my understanding and to help me be of greater service to the congregation.

Meanwhile American mores were in flux, alternate life styles were emerging, divorces zoomed, women became a major part of the business and professional world, intermarriages increased, and the family itself seemed in danger of disintegrating.

My task, it seemed to me, besides the general counseling, was to present the problems of marital relationships from the pulpit and to offer suggestions and solutions. It was not the best response to what was troubling so many, but at least it was a response. My first sermon on the subject was given in 1957 and was called "What Difference Does It Make, We're in Love." It dealt with intermarriage and was the basis of a front page story in the **Minneapolis Tribune** *by Daniel Hafrey.*

Some of the other titles since then were: "When Your Marriage Reaches Its Teens" (1963) which was published in the **American Jewish World,** *in the* **Jewish Digest** *and commented upon by the* **Minneapolis Tribune** *and* **St. Paul Pioneer Press;** *"Why Not Get Married" (1961); "So I'll Get a Divorce" (1967); "The Death of Marriage" (1972); "So You Want To Be Free" (1975); and "Our Greatest Concern" (1978).*

As I reread these sermons, I became acutely aware of the sexist language and the demeaning characterization of women that was so commonplace fifteen and twenty years ago.

The three sermons in this volume are relatively recent ones, but I assure you that my present vocabulary has been greatly altered, and I would never dream now of making some of the "chauvinistic" remarks I was comfortable with when I first began to talk about Marriage and Family.

You may find some repetition in the solutions offered in these sermons. After all, a good answer to a perennial question is still a good answer.

* * * *

The Death of Marriage
January 21, 1976

I am sure there is no need for a long introduction to the topic we are considering this evening. All of us know what is happening. In the country at large, approximately one out of every three marriages ends in divorce. There are no accurate figures, as far as I know, on abandonment, where a parent leaves the family and is not heard from again; or of permanent separation without divorce. And no one knows how many couples — Catholic couples who will not divorce because the Church forbids it, and others, who stay together for a variety of reasons — live in abject misery. Marriage in our society as we have known it, may not be dead, but it is deathly sick.

We Jews used to pride ourselves on our stable families. Among us, divorce was uncommon, separation unusual. It may not have been an ideal family, that most of us come from. Mothers may have been domineering and manipulating, fathers overwhelmed with making a living, but in retrospect it was good and loving and secure. We had a tradition — marriage was kiddushin, a holy relationship. The Shadchan system was unromantic, but it worked. And even in the days of most of our parents, when the Shadchan had given way to love, Hollywood style, most married couples came out of the same neighborhood, from families that knew each other, or of each other, and they joined in similar hopes and goals — goals that somehow were more important than each individual's personal fulfillment or gratification. Marriage was more than indulgence. It was more than sex. Marriage was the basis of a stable home and family and community.

We've Come a Long Way

We've come a long way baby, a long dismal way!

Divorce in the Jewish community is sky-rocketing all over the country. Separation is common. And the interesting thing is that it is almost never bitter. "She's a wonderful mother," he may say to me. Or, "He's a fine human being," she may say. Only rarely do you hear that the break is a result of negligence or infidelity, finances or parental interference. Rather the reason is usually one of self justification. "We have nothing in common any more," they say. "We're not interested in the same things. We have opposite ideas about life and the kids. We're different from when we were married."

Reports indicate that the peak time for divorce in this country is reached within three years of the wedding. For all other marriages, the first two years are the happiest. You would normally think that with the coming of children, the buying of a home, the establishment of roots as a family, the maturing of love, that couples would be drawn even closer together. But it isn't always so. One survey I have seen reveals that though half the wives questioned during their first two years of married life were most content, twenty years later, of those very same wives, only six out of a hundred said they were satisfied and twenty-five percent had become disenchanted with their marriage.

Something had happened in those intervening years, something so destructive to marriage and the family, that a second peak has now been reached in the American divorce courts — those marriages that have endured for twenty to thirty years. And among some of our friends the tendency to disruption has been coming somewhat earlier.

Marital Difficulties

There are many reasons why marriages have difficulty and not the least of them is time — the ordinary passing of time. Most husbands and wives just cannot maintain the rapture, the exhilaration and the absorption with each other that they felt their first few years together, as day follows day, week follows week, and month follows month. It is virtually impossible.

Moreover, the speed in which we live our lives these days can be overwhelming. We look to our marriage for intimacy, for companionship, for understanding. We start out hoping to share our ideals, our beings, our thoughts. We want to grow together, to complement each other, to make of our lives a beautiful unity. But personal growth now proceeds at an ever accelerating rate and the individual development of husband and wife does not always match. A man has his work and the interests that stem from it. A woman has her home, the children, her friends. And there are so many other avenues of interest today that each can choose. Divergences become evident more rapidly these days as we seek to fill our time and express ourselves in the things and activities we enjoy. And as the pace of life quickens, the gap grows. Some of us scarcely notice that we have less and less in common, less and less to talk about, until it may be too late.

Our mores have changed. The kids started it first with the "doing your own thing" bit, and we have taken it over. Freedom of individual action is the watchword of our faith. Add to that the affluence of our times and you have an enemy that many marriages find it impossible to contend with. Moreover, we all know about the variety of different marriage styles being proposed these days. None of these is seemingly for us — as yet — but the very idea of them has helped make divorce and separation more acceptable. In such a milieu, any marriage is vulnerable.

A man finds his income excellent. There are things to do, places to see, people to meet. He is unhappy about the restrictions his home places upon him. The kids may be a problem, the house a nuisance. "Who needs it," he says to himself. "I can afford to keep my wife and the children in the style they have always known. And they won't miss me. I'm not around so very much anyway. And I'll still be able to afford a beautiful pad of my own."

And the ladies are also affected. Some may want to do their own thing, too. They know how good their husband's income is. The children are not infants anymore — or may even be gone. She is still young and attractive. Who knows what may happen? And besides, she won't miss him, she thinks. She'll even enjoy the quiet. The house will be hers, the car and a very adequate income. "Why not?" she says to herself. "It can't be any worse." And she, too, may begin thinking about a lawyer.

And they both rationalize. Though they know the kids may experience some trauma and unhappiness, everyone seems to survive a divorce. And "aren't we all better off away from a quarrelsome home," they say, "with its tensions, its shouting and slamming of doors? Aren't we all better off away from a house where nobody speaks?" And the more they think of it, the less their minds rest on understanding or reconciliation.

Other Factors

There are many factors that lead to estrangement and I cannot list them all here. Everyone of us is aware of them. There is the immaturity of one or both members of the couple, even though they may be 40 years old. He may think she should always be able to wear a size 10, and her few extra pounds have scarred his ego. "This isn't the girl I married," he says to himself. She may think that her body is a weapon, that sex is to be used to reward or punish him, and she does it with calculating cunning. She may expect him to discipline the kids, and he may believe that patience and permissiveness if the answer. Or it may be the other way around. He may be absorbed in his work, striving to achieve, looking for advancement, and she can't stand the way their son looks, or the crowd their daughter is running with. "You don't listen," she says, "when I tell you about them." And he, to please her, explodes when he sees the kids, and feels put upon and guilty thereafter. And even the counsellor-professional or unprofessional may advance the split. As one of them said to me, "I treat the individual, not the marriage. If the marriage is sick, it isn't my responsibility. I want to cure the patient." And that, too, can mean trouble.

Or it comes to this: The goals which they have set for themselves when first they were married have been attained — and there are no new goals. Or the goals which they had hoped to reach now seem far beyond their grasp and there is unspoken disappointment. They just stop talking about what was central in their lives. They live in frustration. Wives growing older need stronger demonstrations of being needed and wanted. Husbands, meanwhile, seem to lose their capacity or forget their propensity to express affection. Whatever it is, their relationship has deteriorated with the onslaught of years.

Marriage and the Future

I don't know what the future of marriage and the family, as we know it, will be. What I do know is that society in general, and Judaism as a way of life, cannot survive their disintegration. It is in the home that a child's character is formed. It is in the home that he learns to love and to live with others. It is in the home that he should learn about Judaism. Business, the public world, brutalizes men and women, often making them callous and insensitive. At home we have an opportunity to be open and honest, we have to share, we have to sacrifice. We learn to rejoice at another's success or happiness, to be hurt by his or her failures. It is not that we need marriage simply for the care and feeding of our children; we need marriage for our own humanizing, to help us attain our most loving and ultimate selves. In the Biblical account Eve is created to be Adam's helpmate. She is more than a woman. She is a wife. And at that moment Adam becomes more than a man. He becomes a husband. They each have someone to care for, someone to need and who needs them. Only then do they really become human. And this has been the Jewish view through the ages — that marriage, the one-to-one relationship between a man and a woman, is the most meaningful relationship that a human being can know.

What Can Be Done?

What can be done to get by the difficult years with the least strain on the marriage? What can be done to avoid the heartaches and aggravation? There are no pills that will do it. There is no set formula. But there are ways that will help.

(1) Keep your eyes on the purpose of your marriage. A happy home cannot abide a selfish mate. You married for your own happiness, it is true, but you have also obligated yourself to be concerned about your partner's happiness. Don't forget it.

(2) There are no married couples that have never argued. There are some arguments that are stupid to begin with; there are some arguments that can never be won. Know when to keep your thoughts to yourself. Not the winning of the argument, but the understanding is what is important.

(3) Don't think you can estrange your partner from his parents and close friends and keep your marriage happy. It won't work.

(4) No one is perfect. No one can be right all the time. Sometimes we mythologize and idealize marriage beyond any sense of reality. Know your partner's limitations and learn to live with them lovingly.

(5) Never forget that your partner has an ego. Just do not take her for granted. If she is lovely in that new dress or has done

something you're proud of, tell her. She trusts your judgment. After all, you asked her to marry you. And ladies, don't take your husband for granted either. His work is never easy. And his ego needs building, too.

(6) Sex is part of any good marriage. But it cannot be used as a favor or as a barnyard activity. His needs are more important than your hair-do. Her feelings may be more important than your needs.

(7) Share your experiences. I have never known a wife who is not interested in what her husband does or whom he meets. Interest yourself in his ideas. And become informed. And men, listening is also a masculine trait. The TV can wait.

(8) Become part of something together. The "Big Show" at Temple was not only fun for me to be in, but what I loved most about it was the sight of so many couples, dancing together, singing together, enjoying each other, working for a common purpose, experiencing something new and exciting together.

(9) Don't let too many years pass without a second honeymoon or third or a fourth. Getting away from the house and from the children, for no matter how brief a period, will give you a chance to concentrate on each other. And you can use it.

(10) Bring some ritual into your household. For example, you can share the Friday evening dinner as no other meal. It will help make you realize that you are a family and belong together.

(11) Don't try to dominate. Don't tell him he is what he is because of you — or vice versa (even though it may be true). Decisions are to be shared. Guidelines for kids should be mutually arrived at and the responsibility for enforcing them is mutual.

"I Love You"

(12) When was the last time you said "I love you." Not in those exact words, they may sound phoney, but with a smile, a gesture, a simple caress. Our forefathers were really so clever. They knew marriage and the family were central to Jewish life. And so they built into our tradition a requirement that at least once a week a woman demonstrated to her husband that she loved him, and a man would tell his wife that she was his world. And both these happenings took place at the same time and the same evening.

Every Friday eve he would go to the synagogue. After the Service, on his arrival home, just as he opened the door to the brightness of his house, as he saw her looking as lovely as she could be, as the aroma of the Shabbat meal which she had lovingly prepared reached him, he would recite to her from the 31st chapter of the Book of Proverbs: "A wonderful wife," he would say,"is what I have, and her worth is far above rubies. The heart of her husband doth safely trust in her. She doeth him good and not evil all the days of her life. Her children rise up and call her blessed. Her husband also, and he praises her (saying), 'Many daughters have done valiantly, but thou excellest them all.' " In other words, he would say, "Darling, I love you" — and she would know that her place as wife and mother was appreciated.

It's just too bad we cannot fall in love with our husbands and wives all over again every single day, but our love need not be corroded by time, nor by the pace we live, nor by our selfishness.

What can we do to avoid the heartaches and the pain? What can we do to put new meaning and life into our marriage? Plenty. Just try.

* * * *

So You Want To Be Free
April 4, 1975

Yesterday afternoon, just after lunch, I ran into a friend with whom I have served on a number of community activities. He stood for awhile admiring my tan in the cold wind, and then he said knowingly, "Where have you been? I haven't seen you for a long time." I told him what you know — that I had been at Florida State University in Tallahassee these past three months studying Marriage and Family Counseling. "Really?" he said somewhat surprised, and then after a moment he asked, "Are there as many divorces in Jewish families as among the population generally — or among the people I know?"

"No," I said, "there aren't. But Jews wherever they live take on some of the aspects of the larger community. Divorces *are* increasing."

And that, of course, is one of the reasons why I went to Florida State. That is one of the reasons why I focused much of my attention there on Divorce Therapy and Remarriage, both of which are new and expanding fields for counselors.

My Concerns

I went to Tallahassee because I was — and am — concerned. My concern is not merely for the people I know, for people who may be part of this congregation — for their lives, their happiness, their families. I am concerned about the society in which we live — for a country that means so much to us. The agony of a discordant marriage is not only a personal tragedy. It reaches to succeeding generations. Psychiatric and social ills, suicide, drug and alcohol abuse, criminality are all possible spinoffs from it. And we have more that our share of these already.

Moreover I am concerned about Judaism and Jewish life. Ours is an adventure in living based primarily on the family. The home has always been the source of Jewish inspiration, education and survival. The synagogue and the school are supplementary, the frosting on the cake. The family is the unit through which Jewish children are socialized, where love and proper living is exemplified, displayed and taught. "Mikdash Me'at" is what the home is called in our tradition — a small sanctuary, a personal sanctuary, where the table is an altar and the parents are the rabbis — the teachers.

You and I know that we have turned much — if not almost all — of the teachings about Jewish life and Judaism over to the synagogues and to other institutions, and we Jews have suffered because of it. But one thing cannot be assigned elsewhere — one responsibility can't be sluffed off. Nowhere else can we — or will we — find the emotional satisfaction, the ongoing security, the individual happiness that the family group provides. Without the family structure, there is no question in my mind that Judaism will atrophy and waste away. It will become a religion of an insignificant people of interest only to historians and anthropologists, and perhaps to psychologists and sociologists.

Our Open Society

We live in a society that is relatively open, where customs change and are changing. We live in a culture that provides most everything material that we could ever want. We want to enjoy. There is enough tragedy and hardship just in living, so we want to make the most and the best of life. We have the time, the affluence and the opportunity to experiment in all kinds of activities, to take a chance. We read *Open Marriage* and we say "why not?" We read that swinging couples love each other more because of it and we say "could be." There is even an eminent psychologist who has written a book called *The Civilized Couples Guide To Extra Marital Adventure* and we say "He should know," or "we are civilized, too."

We do not have exact figures, but between 30 and 40% of all the marriages in this country end in divorce. Fifteen years ago 4% — four out of every one hundred marriages that had lasted fifteen years or more broke up. Today that number is 25%. Twenty-five out of every one hundred marriages of fifteen years or more end in divorce. One writer in a book called *The Spouse Gap* says that when that period comes — when you have been married for fifteen years and more, especially when you reach your forties, wives generally feel neglected, husband unfulfilled. Her life is characterized as Boring, Bourbon, Bridge, and Bonbons. His life, I have added, might be Whiskey, Women, Work, and Whatever.

There are many reasons why marriage, as we know it, is in danger, and we discussed these somewhat last week. The question this evening is not *why* it is in difficulty, but is the basic idea of marriage good? What can be done to improve it? What can a rabbi do? What can a congregation do? What can you who have families do?

Marriage Is Best

I start with the proposition that marriage — and that means monogamy to me — is still the best possible relationship that two people can know. And the fact that there is so much divorce is no reason to think otherwise. Divorce does not reflect a diminished desire to be married. Not at all. It merely indicates that people want to be married, happily. Divorced people are marrying people. And the proof is that most of them do remarry — most of them find a husband or wife again.

And why is marriage so good for us? Why is it best? Look what it provides. Affection and love which all of us need and which no one can live without. It gives us a sense of belonging, companionship, comradeship, someone to be with. It keeps us from being lonely. It provides us with a home and the creature comforts that come with it. There is socially-approved sex, family and children, It is a place where we can find tremendous joy and pride, where you can feel esteemed and wanted, where you can share thoughts and feelings, laughter and sorrow. It can provide an atmosphere where our thoughts can be elevated and stimulated to heights we never dreamed of. It can even be a place where, if necessary, you can get rid of aggression. I think it was Danny Thomas who said, "If you don't fight with your family, you have to fight with strangers."

Many times I stand on this bima — at the Ark — to participate in a marriage. I don't know whether the couple before me, happy, accepted, fulfilled, exhilarated, turned on, has really categorized for themselves all these reasons for marriage. But there they are with every expectation, with every hope, with most every reason to anticipate happiness and contentment. They are in love. And then, two years later you see them, or five years later, or ten years or fifteen and more years. Frustrated. Turned off. Angry. Disillusioned. Bitter. Can these be the same people who vowed to "love, honor and cherish" — "to be consecrated one to the other?" What has happened to their hopes, their dreams, their desire to touch one another, their friendship, their love?

What Has Happened

We know that gaps are inevitable in every marriage. We know that frustration and disagreements arise as the years go on. And we also know that the basic complaint is lack of communication — and this has many forms: "We are not on the same wave length," they say. "Our interests have changed." "We argue when we talk." "We have fallen out of love."

Lack of communication is not the cause of marital ills. It is the result. It is the result of many things: unfulfilled expectations, fantasies unrealized, lack of sexual satisfaction, conflict over children, a deficiency in understanding, a disillusion with oneself or one's partner, no new common goals or anticipations. And I could go on.

And so there are other questions: How do we keep that marriage alive? How can we prevent that marriage from reaching a point of conflict? What can be done before it unfortunately gets there? The answer to that is also what I was searching for these past months.

The subject is so vast. It is so complex, so intricate. It has so many nuances and ramifications. We are each the products of so many different forces and influences. Problems are different at different times in our married lives. And book after book has been written about them. So this is not the time — nor is it possible — to try to give you a five minute remedy for ailing marriages, for split homes, for breaking hearts. There are no pills for such maladies. What I hope to do, is to lead a discussion on these subjects sometime later this year.

What Can Be Done

That is one thing we shall do. And there are others. They may not be a panacaea, but I am convinced they will be helpful.

Marriage, as you know, is a great risk. Joseph Epstein in his book *Divorced in America* has written — "marriage is a contract that is designed to endure long after the point of sexual attraction; it must accomodate itself to the changes in personality wrought by time, be flexible enough to weather failure or success and take all the bumps, slumps and long grey snatches of life that are sufficiently staggering on one's own, but are often doubly dampening when shared."

Now most rabbis — and most clergymen — attempt to point this out to a couple before they are married. We attempt to show them the potholes in the road ahead. And they listen. And they are in love. And they are married. And we really do not see them much again until they have children for Religious School.

That just is not good enough. For many marriages to stay healthy there has to be a continual effort to redefine the marital status — to renegotiate that contract. We change. Roles change. Expectations change. Situations change. Unforeseen problems emerge. They can cause aggravation, anger, acrimony. They have to be understood and even anticipated.

In the past I tried to see a young couple once in the year after they were married, but there was nothing systematic about it. I just sensed it should be done. I did not know just when or how best to do it. Now I have had an opportunity to read the studies. I have had an opportunity to think about it. And we shall devise a system of recalls. We shall devise a means where we can intervene — unobtrusively by ourselves, or at the request of a couple, whenever a crisis or role change occurs. I do not know how many years we may follow a couple or at what intervals — but it makes sense to have a physical checkup annually. So why not a marital checkup?

Then, for those already married for some time. Here the checkup can take a different form. We have had retreats for couples in the past, sponsored by our Men's Club and they have been good. But that, too, was not good enough.

My Hopes

Some months ago, we began a campaign to raise funds for improvements here in the Temple proper and at all our facilities. You heard about it, I am sure. We have a camp. What we had proposed — and you may have seen the brochure — is to build a structure at camp that would house some fifteen couples. Once that is done, besides the family camping we envisage, we hope to take couples out at least once a month for a 24 hour period. Then we shall be able to talk, to open old lines of communication, to renegotiate the marriage contract, to sift through relationships and understandings. And that we will begin to do at our next couples retreat in May.

I also hope — and this is another complicated task — to appeal to the divorce lawyers in town. Now, there are three stages in divorce proceedings. There is the emotional stage, that tense period before the couple decides to separate. There is the separation stage when they first live apart — and there is the final decree. I wish someone could intervene at the emotional stage but that depends on the couple. They have to ask. I hope there can be an intervention at the time of separation and there the lawyers can help.

Our legal system is, as you know, an adversary system. In a divorce procedure too often, and often unwittingly, it sets two fine human beings against one another, frequently with a viciousness and indiscretion that they would never express elsewhere. If a divorce must be, let us help make it as amicable as possible. For no couple can truly break, one with the other, divorced though they may be, if they are held together by animosity. Here we can intervene. Here we can be of assistance — especially if there are children — if the lawyers will help and suggest.

And finally there is divorce therapy. After the decree, adjustment is often necessary. Divorce can be like a death in the family and some of the symptoms that grief brings may appear. Help may be needed not merely for the woman, but for the man as well. Divorce is neither masculine nor feminine. It is a human condition. And here again, lawyers can help.

* * * *

Meanwhile some hints and devices you might try at home:

1. Remember this. You married a unique person. That's why you fell in love. Just go home and ask yourself — and perhaps put the answer on paper — "What are the wonderful things about him that I know? What is it about her that touches me so? How do I really feel? What can I do to show her more of my love?" Let him see what you have written. Let her read what your feelings are. And perhaps you'll talk about them.

2. Take another look at your common goals. What are you seeking together? What were your original hopes? What were you looking for when you stood under the Chupah? Is it a career — or two careers you want? Is it a home, travel, your children's welfare? Are you looking to retirement? What is it that will bring you both happiness?

3. Do you have any common activities? Are there things you can do together — a vacation without the kids or a weekend away? You might take a class together. You might find an organization you can serve together — the B'nai B'rith, the Republican or Democratic Party, the Temple, PTA. Look into it.

4. Keep alive the sense of sexual excitement. And this is appropriate for any age. Remember your spouse has an ego. It likes to be complimented. It can enjoy the spontaneous. And be careful lest you maim or fray it.

5. Reserve time for each other. With the kids, with car pooling, Hebrew School, Little League, tennis, work, and what have you, you may have little time for each other. You may be together but there is no time to talk, to be alone. Set aside some minutes each day, every other day, once a week, when you can talk about what you feel, what you need, what is important to you and in the family.

6. Finally, be ready to forgive. With forgiveness we extend our love to someone who has violated it. In the home it is as loving an act as you can find, as great a solace to the soul as one can imagine.

From my perspective, a good marriage brings human beings as close to happiness and fulfillment as there can be for us here on earth. But creating a good marriage is an art. Its ingredients are much selflessness, much understanding, lots of character, love and effort. And this we all have. Hopefully we can continue to put them all together so that good marriages do not become an art that is lost.

This is where we hope to go. This is what we hope to help you do. May it be so.

Amen

* * * *

Our Greatest Concern
September 21 (Rosh Hashanah), 1978

One hundred years ago, almost to the day, members of 23 Jewish families came together in a hall above a drug store at 213 Hennepin Avenue for the first worship service of what was then known as Congregation Shaari Tov. The Civil War that had devastated the country had ended but 13 years before. Eight years before, the first transcontinental railroad had been completed. The Atlantic and Pacific were now united. A new era of growth and expansion, of booming industry and commerce, of scientific and technical creativity was about to bloom. Minneapolis, recently joined with the village of St. Anthony, was a thriving city of 33,000 people.

That is how and when this congregation, whose name was changed to Temple Israel in 1920, began.

I do not have to tell you what the past 100 years have wrought. From 1890-1914, almost two million Jews poured into this country from out of Eastern Europe. The Atlantic coast was their primary goal but a number made the strenuous trip to Minnesota. They were poor and frightened but education was free and new horizons were spread before them. There were, as we all know, hardships and discrimination; wars that brought tears and pride; buoyant hopes and shattered dreams. There were miracles of human genius, new mores and altered values. There was a Holocaust and also an Israel reborn. And you and I have inherited a world as vastly different from the 1870's as the 1870's were from all other periods of human history that came before them.

More than 23 Jewish families lived in Minneapolis in 1878. How many more I do not know. And I do not know whether an historian would consider the growth of the community to be rapid or slow. By 1882, there were 100 Jewish families in town. Two years later, a second synagogue was founded and four years after that, a third. By the mid-30's, there were some 20,000 Jews in the city and, interestingly enough, that number has not changed to any great extent since then.

The Temple Today

The Congregation of 23, which had expanded to 450 families by 1945, has now grown to some 1750 families. Despite the relatively stable Jewish population, Temple Israel has almost quadrupled in size in the last 33 years. It is, today, one of the largest Reform synagogues in the country. It is no wonder that Matthew Ross, Chairman of the Board of the Union of American Hebrew Congregations, in his remarks at our Centennial Dinner, characterized our congregation as "great."

If we are "great," and I did not press Mr. Ross for his definition; if we are great, I can assure you, it is not because we are big. If we are great, it is not because we have in our membership individuals who have had an impact on American and Jewish life nationally and even internationally. If we are great, it is not because members of the Temple have been in the vanguard of every good and progressive cause in our city, or have had extensive leadership roles in those causes. It is not because its Rabbis have helped shape the community for the last 75 years or that every facet of Jewish and communal life has been made the concern of the congregation. Nor is it because we have an impressive building, or a Camp, an active Sisterhood, Men's Club, and Couples Club, New Horizons, or Youth Programs. If we are great, it is because we are a Reform congregation, because we are liberal.

And liberalism, as you know full well, liberalism today is under attack. It is under attack conceptually, politically, and in the realm of religion, as well.

This was to have been the essence of my remarks to you this Rosh Hashanah Eve. And my point was to have been a simple one. We, at Temple, if *my* voice means anything — we, at Temple, would not abandon our liberal philosophy or tradition. Certainly, we would continue to be open to every new Jewish idea, whether it was dredged up from the past or completely innovative. Certainly, we would continue to experiment and evaluate, but we would not succumb to the pressures from either individuals or community postures as we now begin the next 100 years.

Then, something happened these past few days that made me change what I thought I would say.

The Essential Question

One evening, about a week ago, at some gathering Bernice and I attended, we heard for the first time that a young couple with two beautiful children — a couple we had known and loved — had separated. And that night, as we reflected on the pain we felt, I said to her, "You know, that is really what I should talk about on Rosh Hashanah. That is the most important issue in Jewish life today."

That is what I said, but I had already completed a sermon and was well satisfied with it. And I do not find it easy to write the words I speak from this place.

Then came the next day and more bitter news. Two other young couples, also with children, charming, beautiful, intelligent, had also decided to separate.

My impulse, at that moment, was more rage than sadness. I wanted to come to this pulpit and shout for all to hear: "Enough! This has gone far enough! It has to stop! We have had enough!!"

For, ultimately, the decline, or God forbid, the demise of the Jewish family is the most momentous subject we can consider. There is none of greater concern (not with what is happening) none, whatsoever!! Without the family, Judaism, as a way of life, cannot survive. Without the family, a congregation such as this cannot continue. Without the family, religious schools fall into disuse, volunteerism disappears, interest wanes. Without the family, the next hundred years of Temple history will have little of greatness to it — if, indeed, there is a Temple Israel.

And lest you think I am dreaming, lest you think I am surprisingly and overly pessimistic, listen to this:

Some Statistics

There are some 6,000,000 Jews in this country today. It is an aging population. Its present birthrate does not replace itself. There are defections. And because of all of this, the Harvard Centre for Population Study concluded in a survey it made of the future of the American Jewish population that, "When the United States celebrates its Tricentennial in 2076, the American Jewish Community is likely to number no more than 950,000 persons, and conceivably as few as 10,500" — and that is less than half the number of Jews who live in Hennepin County today.

Talk about our next 100 years! Talk about greatness! Talk about being liberal or Reform! Talk about what is important!

Other Problems

Of course, Israel is important. Of course, we are obligated to give it continuous support and strength. The Camp David agreements with the prospects for peace between Israel and Egypt; the hope of some semblance of stability in the Mideast are among the most important events in our lifetime.

Of course, a commitment to human rights is important. Of course, our involvement in the social problems of our cities and country is essential. Once we Jews were greatly concerned with the restructuring of society. Once we knew that rights for all minorities meant security for us. Today, however, any change in society's structure somehow seems a threat to many among us. But, that kind of credo, inviting as it may be, just cannot be ours. Self interest *only* is one step away from insensitivity. And, that is not the Jewish way. It never has been. It never can be.

Of course, Reform Judaism is important. It is important not only to us, but to all Jewish life. It led Jews from a ghetto mentality and medieval customs into modern culture and contemporary esthetics. It placed women on a par with men in every synagogue activity. It enlightened the non-Jew to the universality of the Jewish message and commitment. It is a barricade against a rejection of the general community and a bulwark against withdrawal into rampant ethnicity.

Ethnicity is in, these days. And, I do not deprecate it for, in many ways, it is very good. But, too often, I see its expression in "shtetl" practices, in a longing and search for Jewish symbolism and identity that is a throwback to what we once discarded as inappropriate and archaic. For some Jews, that is the way. For some congregations, that is the way. But, too often, I see community agencies, agencies that, in concept serve no set Jewish ideology; that profess to be neither Orthodox, Conservative or Reform; who become so zealous in their quest for ethnicity that they engage staff and construct programs that alienate and even eliminate those with a liberal Jewish orientation.

Jewish education is exceedingly important; Russian Jewry is important; as are prayer meetings in executive suites, and the travesty of the Olympic games in Moscow. Of course, we must be concerned with the thin line between abundant energy and anti-Semitism, the single parent family, the Jewish single, and the aged, but there is a primary concern — Jewish survival, healthy, vigorous, meaningful Jewish survival — and it cannot be without Jews. It cannot be without Jewish families.

Israel won't help. Fund raising won't help. Affirmative action won't help. Neither will academic liberalism or psychiatry. Prayer won't help. Somehow, you and I must come to the conclusion that not only our individual welfare has value, but there is value in a Jewish community per se. Somehow, we have to realize that there is a Godly will and mission for us. And for it, we must often sacrifice! For it, we must often sublimate our own satisfactions!

Family Life

I know that some marriages are intolerable and should be terminated. Divorce, in Jewish life, was condoned as far back as Biblical times. I do know that some of us were not meant to be married. I know that many of us can live meaningful and productive lives without a wife or husband or family structure. But, I also know that there is something sacred in the vows made at marriage; the words we speak are not idle words; the promises we make are not given tongue-in-cheek. And, I know, that there is nothing more beautiful, there is nothing that transcends family love.

A marriage is organic. It is a living thing. It must be nurtured and cared for. It cannot exist unattended. And, when a child is born to it, that married couple has to consciously recommit itself to the idea that the family, in and of itself, is important, apart from the proclivities, the disappointments, the individual needs of those who comprise it.

And, no one escapes the hurt when a family dissolves — the individuals, the children, the community, the congregation, Jewish life.

I wish I had a pill that would make marital problems and divorce go away. I wish I had a book or formula or a serum. I wish I could force young couples to truly prepare for their marriage. I wish there were time to sit with them at each anniversary to evaluate and renew their vows. That may be what our congregation may have to do before the next century begins to unfold for us, to develop a marriage clinic with all of the tools of research and counseling. It may be the most worthwhile enterprise we undertake.

For the moment, all I can do is harbor my hurt, prepare a couple as best I can and tell them what I have learned in the years of my own marriage or in my experiences with others who have stood under the chupah. This is what I say, in part:

1. A happy marriage cannot abide a selfish person. Your marriage will not be successful simply because you have found the ideal mate. It will be happy only if you become the ideal mate. And that takes thought. It takes anticipating your loved one's needs, his hopes, her dreams.

2. There are no married couples that do not have their differences. There are some arguments that are stupid to begin with. There are some arguments that can never be won. Know when to keep your thoughts and your words to yourself.

3. No one is perfect. No one can be right all of the time. Know your partner's limitations and learn to live with them lovingly. Be quick to forgive. Be even quicker to ask forgiveness.

4. When you marry, you do not become one. True, you live together, love together, cry together, laugh together. But, you are not one. Your personalities are not meant to be blurred one into the other. They are meant to strengthen each other. You marry not merely for what you each are, but for what you shall become because you are together. You acquire not another you, but a best friend.

5. Become part of something together. For example, soon there will be another "Big Show" at Temple. What an opportunity to work for a common purpose, to dance together, sing together, to enjoy each other, experiencing something new and exciting

together. Do not miss the opportunity.

6. There is a yearning today in our younger generation — a deep spiritual yearning. You should hear the sincere references to God by our Bar and Bat Mitzvahs as they speak each Saturday morning. For them, Israel is not enough. For them, a Seder is not enough. For them, a membership in a congregation, an occasional attendance, a half-hearted attachment is not enough. They want a spiritual relationship. And, primarily, their parents, their grandparents, their families can give it to them. That is a dimension Jewish education and Jewish ethnicity do not necessarily provide. You may learn history and ethics, but not faith. You may learn recipes and ritual, but not spirituality. And besides, none of these is compelling. None of these make a valid framework around which one can order his life. A God directed faith does! — a reaching out beyond oneself; a sense of awe at the miracle of life and nature; a wonderment at the capacity to love that we possess, a groping for the Infinite, a heart attuned to its command.

Renewed Hope

Each year begins for us Jews not merely with a new day but with a renewed hope. Each Rosh Hashanah tells us that the past is available to us to review, to examine, to savor if we wish, to abandon or to build upon. A New Year is before us — 365 clean, beautiful, unmarked days. What a magnificent gift!! What a scintillating challenge!!

May each and every day be one filled for you with love, with cheer, with good health and contentment.

And grant us the will, O Lord, the desire, the zeal and the courage that our homes and our beloved congregation may grow from strength to strength, that one hundred years from now, our children, our grandchildren and our great grandchildren may also say, "Thank You, O Lord, for all of Thy goodness to us."

Baruch ata Adonai Elohaynu Melech ha'olam,
she-he-che-ya-nu, v'ki-y'ma-nu, v'hi-gi-a-nu laz'man ha-zeh.

Praised be Thou, O Lord our God, Ruler of the Universe, who has kept us alive, who has sustained us and permitted us to reach this blessed day.

Amen

The Andrew Young Affair

September 21 (Rosh Hashanah), 1979

I sent you "The Andrew Young Affair" soon after I gave it from the pulpit on Rosh Hashanah, 1979. I include it in this volume as a reminder that though Andrew Young has been quiet and Jesse Jackson somewhat stifled, their commitment to the P.L.O. and the problem of Black-Jewish relationships in this country will not soon disappear.

* * * *

This year is somewhat of a milestone for me: I am now in my 25th year as a rabbi. It does not seem so long ago, though it was December 19, 1954, that I first came to Minneapolis for an interview with a pulpit committee and with the Board of Trustees of the Temple. The following June, immediately after I was ordained as a Rabbi, Bernice and I and our children came back to make it our home. This coming March my rabbinic classmates and I will gather once again in Cincinnati to receive Doctor of Divinity Degrees from our Seminary, the Hebrew Union College. They will be honorary Degrees, and it is the way our school recognizes those of us who have persevered in the rabbinate for a quarter of a century.

And each year as I have come to this pulpit on Rosh Hashanah, I have tried to evaluate the status of Jewish life, to express my concerns, to ascertain, appraise, and apprize you of some matter that is significant not only to you as individuals, but to the total Jewish community. As you know, crisis has not been foreign to us these past 25 years; and each Rosh Hashanah our world seems more frenetic, our American society more enigmatic, our Jewish existence more complicated. And this year is no different — perhaps even a little more so. This year may well be a watershed year for the American Jewish community, the beginning of changes we never dreamed of. I refer to what has taken place, and what is taking place, as an aftermath to the Andrew Young Affair.

The Resignation

You and I do not have to review the course of events that led to Young's resignation. We need not discuss whether he was a good or poor Ambassador, whether his judgements were inane or perceptive, whether he was a liability or an asset, whether he was a diplomatic disaster or not. Much has been said — and can be said — on both sides.

We need not discuss whether he was spied upon and bugged or whether he was not spied upon and bugged; whether his conversation with the P.L.O. representative was an unspoken Jimmy Carter policy or was done on his own initiative. What seems clear to me is that had he not been black, he might well have been dismissed many times before. This time he lied. This time the embarrassment was more than the Carter administration could take. It could forgive mistakes. It could forgive his derogatory statements about his own country. It could forgive his insults to other nations, his skewed assessment of foreign leaders, but it could not condone a lie — a lie by an Ambassador to his superior. My guess is that Secretary of State Vance must have breathed a sigh of relief.

The Israeli Reaction

Nor need we talk about the ineptitude of the Begin government and the machinations of the Carter administration as the episode unfolded. That Young had told his Secretary of State one story and the Israeli ambassador another, you all know. What you may not know is that he also asked Israel to keep the true account secret.

But for reasons of its own, perhaps unable to assess the consequences, unsuspecting, as most of us were, of the seething resentments in the black community, the Israeli government made one of its most unfortunate diplomatic decisions. It decided to go public.

Black Leaders React

I do not know what came first, the sensational headlines in the *New York Post* screaming "Fire Him" and "Jewish Fury at Lie by Young" or the angry response of some black spokesmen who, without seeking the facts, bitterly accused Israel and American Jewry of demanding Young's ouster. They then stoked their bitterness by denouncing Jews for their positon on affirmative action, particularly the DeFunis, the Bakke and Weber cases.

That Israel and American Jewry did not demand Young's resignation did not sway them. That Jews did not create the

DeFunis, Bakke or Weber cases did not deter them. That Jews had been on both sides of these issues did not interest them. That the Jewish concern was not with Andrew Young, the Ambassador, but with the integrity of U.S. foreign policy did not bother them. The voices were strident and shameless. On such distortions do demagogues feed.

The Administration Reacts

A sentence or two from Secretary Vance or President Carter could well have scotched this rising fury at its onset. The truth, from either one of them, could well have put an end to these blatant accusations. But what did the President and his Secretary do? Cyrus Vance went off to Martha's Vineyard for vacation. Jimmy Carter took his trip down the Mississippi.

What can one say to such insensitivity? It portrays an Administration that is either incredibly insensible and completely unaware of the mood of the country; or so sophisticated and sly as to conceive and create the kind of Machiavellian scenario that has developed. Here is how it goes: a troubled White House, by its silence, infers that it was not the President and Secretary of State who want to replace the highest ranking black leader in the Administration. Rather it is the Jewish community — the Jewish people — always such a useful scapegoat. What an ingenious way for removing political pressure and saving the black vote. What a subtle scheme, to encourage a frustrated black community to turn its anger away from an Administration that has failed to curb inflation. What a ploy by a Presidential staff that has done little to reduce ghetto unemployment. Channel the anger toward the Jews. Get the blacks off our backs. What a convenient outlet! Jews are so easy to identify and so easy to hate. And they are so vulnerable.

The Aftermath

Some weeks later, when the President did get around to mentioning the rift, it was already too late. What he said did nothing to alleviate the situation. The momentum had already set in. For while the President had been travelling the Mississippi, there were meetings of all kinds. National Jewish leaders met in New York. So did black leaders. Jewish leaders met with Andrew Young; black leaders with P.L.O. supporters. And Jewish and black leaders met together, both on a national level and in many communities throughout the country.

Though some of the black leadership understood that Andrew Young's resignation was not a black-Jewish problem, and that Jews and blacks did not have to see eye to eye on every issue, a radicalized, more vocal group emerged, a group more turbulent and troublesome and more exploited by the media. I did not see a Bayard Rustin or a Vernon Jordan of the Urban League on television. I saw a posturing Jesse Jackson and a Joseph Lowery. It made no difference that they had little knowledge of the history and complexity of the Middle East. They were the ones to bring it stability and peace. Humorist Art Buchwald, in one of his columns, found it laughable. But it was no laughing matter.

For when, on August 21, Rev. Joseph Lowery and members of his Southern Christian Leadership Conference met with some National Jewish leaders, black resentment, anger and hostility were evident and expressed. And when on the same day some 200 black representatives from virtually all the black organizations in the country came together, anti-Semitic remarks were not uncommon. At the conclusion of this meeting, Jesse Jackson grabbed the microphone and exclaimed, "My wife has just returned from seeing Arafat, and I've been invited to meet him with a delegation of civil rights leaders. Anyone that wants to come with me, just sign up." And he was deluged with requests.

Where Are We?

So where are we?

In cities such as ours, the initial uproar and impact has been diffused. On a national level, a quiet seems to have settled in. But the fallout is in the making, and our Jewish communities, both locally and nationally, face a situation they have never known before. It is not of black anti-Semitism I speak. A recent Gallup poll indicates that 78% of the black population has a friendly attitude toward Jews. It is not that at all. What is new, what is different, what is dangerous, is that now, for the first time, the P.L.O.— still pledged to the destruction of Israel, still pledged to kill Jews — has a voice and a constituency in this country!

You know what has happened the last two days. Lowery and his people have met with Arafat and have been refused a meeting with the Israelis. Jackson is on his way to Beirut, and Israel has refused to talk with him. Meanwhile Andrew Young is reported to be forming a non-profit group to promote the black view on national and foreign affairs. It takes little imagination to envisage a black constitutency, with Andrew Young as its foreign affairs expert and with Palestine as their foreign policy platform. The P.L.O.will be given a built-in, powerful, front-page, prime time American protagonist, such that money could never buy. And funds will not be lacking. Libya's Col. Quaddafi, who has only Billy Carter in tow these days, now has a windfall, unexpected and exultant. And the State Department — or Jimmy Carter — will no longer be at a loss to find a domestic lobby to challenge whatever influence Jewish groups may have.

One Thing More

And one more thing. In championing the cause of the P.L.O., Andrew Young will be speaking not only for his own following and State Department Arabists, but for a growing segment of the American public, that may be committed to Israel, but which feels that the only solution in the Middle East lies with a State dominated by Arafat and his retinue.

The P.L.O. is not going to disappear. Arab wealth is not going to vanish. The energy crisis will not soon be solved. Jesse Jackson, Rev. Lowery and Andrew Young will not go away no matter how much we may wish it. And Israel will be beset. It will be on the defensive as never before. It will not be guns and armies besieging it. That, thank God, it can defend against. It will be verbal attacks, more powerful and shocking than we have ever heard. It will be in its corroding prestige in the Congress, within the Defense Department, in the White House. It may be in party platforms. It could be at the polling places.

And the American Jewish community, you and I, will be on the defensive as never before, justifying Israel actions, explaining her policies, responding to accusations. And the hate mongers, the hate mongers will not be far from the scene.

Our Reactions

How do we react to this emerging and impending omen? What can we do in concert or individually? I am sure that minds more astute than mine, more experienced than I, are struggling for answers. Here are mine. Take them for what they are worth.

1. We must be very sure who our antagonist is. It is not the black community, no matter what Young, Jackson or Lowery may say or do. The black community is not monolithic. It does not speak with one voice, though that is all we seem to be

hearing. There are minds that think more clearly; there are statements that are more thoughtful; there are perspectives that have greater insight.

So to those who speak in the tones of Jackson, we can point out the illogic of their rhetoric, the immorality of their stance, the fallacy of their facts. They may not listen, others may not listen — but we shall be heard. With those who talk like Bayard Rustin, we must continue the pursuit for peace and justice. And with the entire black community, we hopefully will rekindle our cooperation, to bring a better life to those without work, with poor education and inadequate homes.

For too long has our Jewish voice been muted; for too long have our Jewish sights been preoccupied. Somehow we felt rejected as black leadership took over the struggle for human rights, a struggle we felt was ours, too. Many of us thought their demands were self-defeating: quotas was their byword; the merit system sustained us. But strangely enough we need one another. Uncaring, angry, we prosper our mutual enemies. We who walked side by side in the 60's, we whose lives were threatened for the cause of freedom; we who thrilled as hearts sang out "We Shall Overcome" — we cannot turn our backs now on what was right and just then, and what is still right and just today.

The Enemy is the P.L.O.

2. The enemy is the P.L.O., its terror tactics, its avowed determination to destroy Israel; its inherent criminality and villainy. And you and I, and all people should know who they really are — who these people, espoused by the Jacksons and Lowerys, really are. We should be able to tell our friends — our Jewish and our non-Jewish friends — that these terrorists acquire their skill for their indiscriminate killings in Russia — read the current *New York Magazine* if you will — and they shall bring with them a new Russian presence into the Middle East. What does Jesse Jackson, who worries so much about American dependence on Arab oil, make of that?

We should be able to tell our friends, our Jewish friends and those who are not Jewish, that no recognized Arab leader in the Middle East wants a P.L.O. state. Even President Carter admitted that. Do you know that in Saudi Arabia and Kuwait there are regulations keeping P.L.O. Palestinians from rights accorded others. Do you know that they cannot operate in or from Egypt, that they are totally banned in Jordan, that they are kept under strict control in Syria. Only in Lebanon, which they have virtually destroyed, are they free to operate, and even there, a Christian opposition is ranged against them.

We should be able to tell our friends that the P.L.O. has assassinated American diplomats, that it is linked to other vicious terrorists in Germany and Italy, that it has killed or beaten West Bank Palestinians who want to accommodate with Israel. We should be able to tell our friends that there is never an excuse for bombs in market places, deliberately timed to kill men and women and children.

Are these the kind of people whom we, or our friends — or Jackson and Lowery — want to associate with? Are these the kind of people our Administration would want to support?

3. The government of Israel is not sacrosanct. Its decrees do not come from Sinai. It is plagued by internal problems. Its Orthodox parties seem oblivious to what is right, necessary and prudent not only domestically but in foreign matters. Decisions are sometimes made that you and I cannot honestly defend. Let us say so. Let us not be constrained when honest we must be. But let us never obscure what is basic: Israel's security and survival. Whatever threatens that is unacceptable to us. Whatever threatens that threatens us.

4. We must continually strengthen and undergird our own communities. That is a glib and commonplace statement. It is used to sell bonds and to gather pledges for the Federation. It has been made in this sanctuary many times before, and, I suspect, it has been said in every synagogue everywhere in the world. Each speaker has his own agenda. Each speaker has his own conception of community. Each speaker has his own notions of what needs strengthening and how. I have mine. Perhaps we shall share them on Yom Kippur . . .

Let Us Remember

Meanwhile let us remember that we Jews have always been the conscience of the world. It is the Torah that proclaimed, "Justice, justice shall you pursue" and "Love your neighbor as yourself." It was our prophets who declared, "Have we not all one Father," and "The work of righteousness shall be peace." It was the Psalmist who wrote, "How good and how pleasant it is for brothers to live together in unity." Those words are — or should be — emblazoned on our hearts. We do not know what the New Year will bring, but we have always lived with hope and optimism, with faith in God and the promise in humankind. And that is how we face the days ahead.

"Zochraynu L'Chaim, Melech hofez bechayim. Remember us unto life, O Thou who delightest in life" — that is the essence of our prayers this Rosh Hashanah Eve. And may the year to come fulfill our hopes and our prayers — and bring to us and all people contentment and peace,

> *peace in our homes,*
>
> *peace in our lives,*
>
> *peace in our world,*
>
> *that peace for which we all yearn,*

Amen

The Israel Dilemma
September 12 (Rosh Hashanah), 1977

I need not tell you, I am sure, that Israel, though a democracy, is a theocratic state in one essential way. Though all religions are recognized, protected, and free to exist, Reform and Conservative Judaism are discriminated against.

Despite the fact that the overwhelming preponderance of Jews in the United States are Reform and Conservative in their religious affiliations and that it has been through them primarily that help to Israel has been given, relatively few of us have been willing to criticize the politicized Israeli Orthodox establishment for fear of weakening Israel's position in the world.

As I write this, things are getting better and worse. One of the Reform congregations in Tel Aviv has been given permission to build a building, something they could not obtain before, and three Reform rabbis have challenged the Orthodox hierarchy by performing a marriage. Such an act is "illegal" in Israel, but the three men are prepared to go to jail for their beliefs and take the matter through the Israeli judicial system up to the Supreme Court. That is the "good." The "bad" is that last Rosh Hashanah (1979), the Chief Rabbi of Jerusalem decreed that anyone who listened to the shofar in a Conservative congregation — and that meant Reform, too — had not fulfilled the mitzvah of listening to a shofar. In other words, those congregations were not Jewish. So there you have it.

I talked about the issue many times. The last time was on Rosh Hashanah, 1977.

* * * *

Forty-nine years ago, almost to the day, this building was dedicated. It was a work of love by its architect, its builders and all those who planned and watched it rise from the ground. Twenty years ago, again almost to the day, the Sanctuary was reconstructed. The Bima was expanded and changed; the seating altered; the Ark and the choir loft remodeled.

And when, God willing, we reach the 100th anniversary of our congregation some nine months from now (at our next annual meeting), the current renovation will be complete — the balcony seats will be upholstered; the new organ and doors installed; the lecturns, pulpit chairs, the Ark and Torah covers redone; and initial miscalculations — whatever they may be — rectified. And, again God willing, this congregation will be able to look forward to at least another half-century here in this building on this spot.

A Tense Summer

I must tell you that primarily because of the renovation, this has been a tense summer for me. Every morning as I would come into the Temple, I would walk into the Sanctuary to see what was happening. Every evening as I left I would take another peek. And often I would just step in during the afternoon and look and look and look. Each day I had new apprehensions. I just could not imagine how it would be, after the twelve weeks of painters, carpenters and electricians. I would wake up at night worried whether the carpet would be appropriate, the color of the seats proper, if the lighting would have the right effect, if the sound system would be adequate.

I would wander amid the scaffolding and rubble and wonder if we would be ready on time. I agonized whether, with all the demands of the new safety regulations, we could seat you all, for the two times each year when everyone on our Temple roster seems to be present. And now that I stand at this lectern and I look out to you and the Sanctuary is full and colorful and beautiful, not only do I breathe a silent, sobering, heartfelt sigh of relief, but I say for all of us:

Baruch Atta Adonai Elohenu Melech Ha-olam Shehecheyanu, V'kiyimanu V'higiyanu Lazman Hazeh.

Praised be Thou, O Lord our God, Ruler of the Universe, Who has kept us alive, Who has sustained us and Who has permitted us to reach this meaningful day . . .

A Disturbing Summer

It has been a tense summer and in many ways a disturbing one. I have had my bout with the *Star-Tribune* concerning massage parlors and saunas; I have watched the rise of a new anti-Semitism in Germany and Argentina and the alarming growth of the strength and influence of the Arab world. The abortion issue has been aggravated by Federal action and Catholic Church activity; the problem of unemployment in the large cities has been frightening to me. I am ambivalent and concerned about Mena-chem Begin's words and actions in the foreign affairs of his country — and just the other day there was that dismaying advertisement in the local press.* I thought about talking on that issue this evening, but it seemed to me that to speak about Jesus on a Jewish Holy Day was a *Hillul Hashem* — was unseemly. I just could not do it. So I shall address myself to that subject at the first opportunity after the holidays. Tonight there is a different problem — one over which we may have greater control — that I want to discuss with you.

Judaism in Israel

In the State of Israel, for religious purposes, the Jewish people are divided into two groups: one called "dati," the Orthodox, those who follow Halacha, ancient Jewish law; and the "lo dati," all the others, and these make up about 75% of the population. Some weeks ago the *Jerusalem Post*, that great Israeli newspaper for the English-speaking public, printed a revealing cartoon about the two of them. This is how it went:

There are two men — a "dati" and a "lo dati" and the latter has his head buried in a newspaper. "Listen to this," the lo dati (the non-Orthodox) says, and he reads from the paper: "Jews have been denied land for a synagogue."

"What?" screams the dati. "Those anti-Semitic Russian swine! Organize a protest march! Hand me the phone! Which embassy do we picket?"

The lo dati continues from the paper, and this is what he reads: "The Tel Aviv municipality turned down such a request by a group of Reform Jews by a vote of six to four."

The dati listens, stares accusingly at the reader, and blurts out, "What are you, some kind of troublemaker?"

Who Is A Jew

Well, I want to be a troublemaker this Rosh Hashanah evening if I can. I have to be a troublemaker, if trouble is what my words provoke. I have kept from speaking on this matter far too long. But now it is time. There will be none better for years.

And the issue to which I speak is not merely the paranoid Orthodox opposition to Reform Judaism in Israel — and Conservative Judaism, as well —but is something far more fundamental. It is a question of who is a Jew. It is a question of who is a

---

*The "Jews for Jesus" full page advertisement in the *Minneapolis Star*.

rabbi. It is a question of who determines what in Jewish life, on whose authority, on what basis and how.

In Israel, as you know, there is a Law of Return, which states that anyone who is a Jew, upon application, can immediately become an Israeli citizen with all its rights and privileges. Because of Israel's political structure and Ben Gurion's desire for unity, it was given to the Orthodox rabbinate to determine who exactly was a Jew. That meant according to the stipulation in the Halacha, regulations which we Reform Jews do not consider binding. It also meant that only those born of a Jewish mother or converted to Judaism by a recognized Orthodox rabbi (i.e., one recognized by the religious establishment in Israel) would be considered to be Jewish.

I am not going to go into all the hardships and suffering this has caused among the survivors of Nazism, among the refugees from Russia and other lands, or to some Israelis who were native born. In a number of cases it was blatantly inhumane. But that was the law. And Israel was always in danger. So, though there was a protest from American Jews now and again, no one really dared to speak out, no one wanted to say much, for fear that you and I might give less to Israel's support. And so our disappointment, our concern, our pain was hidden — the matter somehow swept under the table.

Agitation For Change

Yet there was agitation by the liberal element in the Knesset and by the Reform rabbis in Israel. And in 1970 the law was changed. Now individuals who had become Jewish under Reform or Conservative auspices were recognized as Jews. Now the position we Reform Jews have always held — that a child with one Jewish parent, brought up as a Jew, was in fact a Jew. Now this had credence in Israel, as well as in the rest of the world.

· And this brings us to the present situation.

Menachem Begin, unlike any of the previous Israeli prime ministers, is an Orthodox Jew. His hold on his office rests on the votes of the Orthodox political parties in Israel. One of his promises to them — and one of his initial proposals as Prime Minister — was a commitment to introduce a bill reverting to the original Law of Return. The slight recognition given Conservative and Reform Judaism was to be taken away. The thousands of women converted by Reform and Conservative rabbis over the years, their children and grandchildren, even great-grandchildren, were, now at the behest of the Israeli rabbinate and a vote of the Knesset, to be stripped of their identity as Jews. How many of them had given of their wealth, their energy, perhaps their lives for Israel we shall never know. The whole idea was — and is — preposterous, offensive, even vile. But it seemed that Begin had the votes to do it.

This time the reaction from Conservative and Reform leadership was immediate and sharp. When Mr. Begin came to visit with President Carter, he also met with two representatives from each group. One of them was Rabbi Stanley Rabinowitz, whom many of you remember and who is now president of the Rabbinic Assembly. Another was Rabbi Ely Pilchik, president of the CCAR, a dear friend and one with whom I communicate frequently. This is what Rabbi Pilchik had to say about the meeting in New York with Mr. Begin:

"I pleaded with Mr. Begin not to undermine the semicha (ordination) of Reform and Conservative rabbis. I reminded him of the role played by Stephen S. Wise, Abba Hillel Silver and now Alex Schindler in building and sustaining the state. He was astonished to learn that Abba Hillel Silver was a Reform rabbi. He had never known it. He did not seem to be informed about our movement and its Zionist role. We informed him that a viable solution had been worked out with Golda Meir when she was prime minister in 1970. He did not know about this."

The four rabbis traveled to Israel in mid-August to talk with Mr. Begin and his staff once again. Now, reports Rabbi Pilchik, Mr. Begin was searching for some kind of compromise, even though his advisors were not. The visitors met with the Orthodox rabbinate in Israel and they had a most unpleasant meeting with Rabbi Goren, the Ashkenazi Chief Rabbi. He sought to divide the Conservative from the Reform spokesmen. "Reform rabbis enjoy eating ham," he said, "and besides, how could anyone who rides on the Sabbath conduct a proper conversion."

The trip of the American rabbis included radio interviews and much press coverage, as well as lobbying with the leaders of all the Israeli political parties. "It was very difficult," Rabbi Pilchik told me the other day. "It was somewhat embarrassing, but I am now certain that if Begin introduces the bill, it will never pass."

My Commitment To Israel

Now my personal commitment to Israel is no less today than it was before Mr. Begin became prime minister. But a commitment to Israel does not mean an uncritical support of all of its policies. In the area of foreign affairs, I can only venture opinions. The analysts, historians and commentators are far more competent than I. In matters of economics, I am a novice. Military strategy is not one of my strong points. But when distinguished rabbis, representing the vast preponderance of American Jews, must travel to Israel to plead with its government for Jewish rights there, then I must speak out. When a Jewish state, as Israel claims to be, discriminates against Jews, who can be silent? When a rabbi in Johannesburg, South Africa, can say of Begin's policy: "This is like Jews making other Jews wear the yellow star," you know how profound the feelings are — that this is no casual matter in Jewish life. It touches to the core of the kind of a state Israel is to be. It touches to the core of Israel/Diaspora relationships. It touches ultimately on the survival of Israel.

That survival is vital to everyone of us. No one has to belabor the point. We all know Israel depends on our help financially, morally, politically. We all know that there can be no pause in our solid and steadfast support. We all know we have to continue to contribute as much as we can and more. That is a given. That is a fact.

What Do We Do

So what do we do, you and I, in the face of this dilemma: on the one hand we know Israel must have as much support as we can give; at the same time we know we must oppose this preposterous policy. There are a few options available to us, it seems to me:

We can advocate Aliyah. I, and liberal rabbis all over the country, can urge, recommend, try to persuade people like you to move to Israel. Then, as the scenario goes, when there are enough of us there, our voices and votes will count and we will change the official religious climate. That solution is obviously not only foolhardy, it is self-defeating. I do not believe in Aliyah for myself — how could I have the audacity to try to prevail upon you. And all of us know that Israel's well-being depends on a strong American Jewry. We need to build a vigorous future here, if there is to be a vigorous future there.

We can go along as we have been. You and I can say: "What

they do in Israel does not bother me. It does not affect my life."
We shall give to the Federation. Whenever we are asked for funds
to help Reform institutions in Israel, we shall give that, too. So
let's go along the way we have been. Eventually it will all work
out!" But that is no answer either.

We can insist that every Federation of every American city
communicate with the prime minister, demanding that the
religious hierarchy in Israel recognize the rights of Reform and
Conservative Judaism and the validity of their rabbis. That I shall
try to do in our city. What effect it will have, I do not know, but
at least it will indicate to Mr. Begin and his cabinet where
American Jews really stand. Perhaps he will learn something.
Perhaps it will give him pause to reflect. But this also is no
answer.

ARZA

We can join ARZA.

ARZA is a new word for many of you. I hope it becomes a
familiar one. It means the Association of Reform Zionists in
America.

ARZA is the most recently created mass membership organization on the American Jewish scene. It is affiliated with the Union
of American Hebrew Congregations and is open to all Reform
Jews. It was established this past year with one purpose only: to
join the World Zionist Organization, to become involved in its
decision making process, and to speak up on behalf of Reform in
Israel. At present the only religious influence in the WZO, that
powerful, overarching zionist organization, is the Mizrachi, an
Orthodox group tied to the Orthodox religious party in Israel. At
no time heretofore has there been a liberal spokesman. Now with
ARZA we shall have one. Now we shall have a voice — and
hopefully a powerful one.

I am urging you to join ARZA, for only through a large
membership can its impact truly be felt. A number of you have
already joined. So have I. And the process is very simple — an
application will appear in one of the forthcoming bulletins. And it
may well be that because of you and me and ARZA, because of
people like us, Israel will take that long-awaited step toward
becoming the country we all want it to be — a 20th century state
in every facet of its existence.

A New Year

This evening we begin a new year in our lives. It is a time for self-examination. We ask ourselves those simple but searching questions that we must ask each year. What kind of person have I been? Really, what kind? What kind of husband, wife? What kind of parent, child? What kind of brother, sister, employer, employee? What kind of Jew? What have I done this past year that has been truly worthwhile? We ask the questions not as an academic exercise — we ask them and we sit in judgement of ourselves.

May you judge yourself with honesty, humility and satisfaction. May you rejoice with your families. May you delight in good health and contentment in the months and years to come.

May God bless you all with plenty, with love, and with peace.

Amen

The Rabbi's Message

As you know, the Rabbi's Message is a short column that appears in every issue of our Temple News.

I have used the Rabbi's Message as a special vehicle for reaching the entire congregation, and I have written it as if I were writing a personal letter to each of you. The subjects ranged from private piques to just plain musings; from innovations I wanted to announce, to international problems. Here is just a sampling.

The Merchant of Venice

January 2, 1974

The "message" on the Merchant of Venice, mild though it was in comparison to the sermon discussing it, caused much consternation at the Guthrie Theatre. Will Thorkelson, Religious Editor of the **Minneapolis Star,** *saw the "message" and wrote a piece on it for his paper. The Associated Press picked it up and* **Variety,** *the entertainment paper, followed with a story.*

I have had one other confrontation with the Guthrie Theatre, but I did not make it public. And despite my occasional disappointments with the Theatre, I have continued to support it financially. As for "Merchant of Venice," I doubt whether it will be repeated by Guthrie, and I trust no other theatrical group in the community will attempt to perform it.

* * * *

I went to see the Guthrie production of "The Merchant of Venice" the other evening.

I have been an enthusiastic supporter of the Guthrie Theatre from the time it was founded. I participated in the moving ceremony when it opened. I have seen every play. But this time I went with a somewhat different feeling than ever before.

A number of you had mentioned that you have been disturbed by the current production. Some told me you would not go to it as a form of protest. A student in our Confirmation Class said she felt "stared at" during the performance. And, of course, I wanted to see for myself how the play had been produced and staged.

I shall save my full comments for Friday evening, January 4, but I must make an observation here. Though the production is an excellent one, though it is staged beautifully and moves swiftly, though the character of Shylock is portrayed with as much dignity as may be possible, though I shall certainly continue to support the Guthrie Theatre, the selection of this particular play as part of its repertoire was, in my estimation, a great mistake in judgement.

We have taken our Confirmaton Class to "The Merchant of Venice" and tried to prepare its members for what they were to see. I am looking forward to discussing it with them. First reports indicate that their reactions did not differ markedly from mine.

As ever,

The Governor's Prayer Breakfast
May 8, 1972

I do not object to the public Governor's Prayer Breakfasts though I have not attended in years. One reason is that at such meetings I am sometimes the unwilling and unwitting witness to statements such as the one I wrote about in this Rabbi's Message.

What I do object to are those private sectarian breakfasts that our present governor (Governor Quie) has had with members of government, business, etc. Even though these breakfasts are not an official government project, nothing that the governor does with any of his constituency is "a-political." And prayer breakfasts do discriminate.

* * * *

I don't know how many of you saw the account of the Governor's Prayer Breakfast in the *Minneapolis Star* some days ago. About 800 people were in attendance and besides the usual Bible readings, prayers and songs they heard a talk by Virginia Congressman G. William Whitehurst.

According to the story, Congressman Whitehurst said, "The two great commandments were given by Jesus. 'Thou shalt love the Lord thy God with all of thy heart, with all of thy soul, with all of thy mind, and with all of thy strength' and 'Thou shalt love thy neighbor as thyself.'"

I wonder how many of you, how many of those at the Breakfast, or how many people who read the story, know that this is a most common bit of misinformation. Both statements are from the Torah. "Thou shalt love the Lord" etc., is in the Book of Deuteronomy (6:5), and "Thou shalt love thy neighbor" etc., is in the Book of Leviticus (19:18), and both were written at least 500 years before Jesus.

I have sent a note to Congressman Whitehurst and also to the *Star* not out of any chauvinism or the "we said it first" syndrome. I don't know whether editors feel obligated to indicate obvious factual mistakes made by speakers whose words their papers report, but certainly the Congressman should be made aware of the inaccuracy.

And as for "who said it first," that matters little. What matters is that all of us live as if those two commandments really do matter.

As ever,

The Viet Nam War

I became disenchanted with the war relatively early. I did my protesting at various public meetings, but that was a personal matter and I did not speak about it from the pulpit until Rosh Hashanah 1967. The response was mixed, part hostile, part cheering.

In 1973 at another of those public meetings, I was asked to make a "confessional." I wrote it as I would have for a Yom Kippur Service and I made it part of my Rabbi's Message for January 16 of that year. This is it.

* * * *

We come here in contrition, in hurt and in shame. We come as Americans, proud of our heritage, humiliated by our callousness. We come here to cry out, to protest, to share our sorrow and disgrace.

The innocents are slaughtered and our eyes are dry.

The fatherless call for help and we bring them greater pain.

The dead and dying assail us and we close our ears, harden our hearts and turn aside.

Forgive us, O Lord. We are a people who have lost our way.

We confess that brutality has desensitized us.

And we ask Thy forgiveness.

We confess our reluctance and our inability to make our spokesmen hear our pleas.

And we ask Thy forgiveness.

We confess our insensitivity to ruthlessness. We confess our inhumanity. We confess that we have shunned Thy word, though our leaders invoke Thy name! We confess that we are killers.

And we ask Thy forgiveness.

Forsake us not. Give us the will to overcome the evil we know. Strengthen our resolve that bloodshed may stop and that nations may no longer lift up swords against nations nor know war anymore.

Now presumably, negotiations have begun again. Now may the new year bring us peace.

Amen

Saunas, Massage Parlors
and the *Minneapolis Star-Tribune*

You may recall that not very long ago the **Minneapolis Star-Tribune** *accepted advertisements from saunas and massage and rap parlors. That policy has now changed, but the decision was at least two years in the making.*

As you can see from the first of the two columns following, I began the move for change in a most unobtrusive way. I knew that my own efforts would have little effect so I asked Msg. Francis Fleming and Dr. Jerald Jackson, both colleagues, to join me for lunch with the publisher and advertising manager of the paper. Though we had little response from them, a column by Msg. Fleming in his church publication caught the eye of the Star's religious editor, and soon a large segment of the community was aroused.

That was not the end of the matter by any means. It took much more prodding, and the result, it seems to me is a far more responsible press and a considerably more appropriate family newspaper.

* * * *

. August 2, 1977

Some weeks ago I initiated a meeting between myself and two of my colleagues (Msgr. Fleming of St. Olaf's and Rev. Jackson of Hennepin Methodist) with the publisher and advertising manager of the *Star* and *Tribune*. The purpose: to discuss our concern with the sauna, massage and rap parlor advertisements in their papers.

I am sure most of you have seen the newspaper account. The result was a change in advertising policy by the *Star/Tribune*. It was, however, a change in which I was most disappointed.

If you recall, the press quoted me as saying that the new policy "was a good first step." That was before I had seen how it actually affected the ads.

Now I have seen the "directory listing" of the advertisements and from my perspective the new policy is neither good nor a firm step. It is a hobble and a very poor one at that. It smacks of hypocrisy and verbal sleight of hand. I am more convinced than ever that such advertisements have no place in any newspaper.

Though the salacious language now is missing, the ads appear to have even greater prominence than before the change. They belie the far-sighted and responsible approach to the community that the *Star/Tribune* has taken on so many other matters. I wish the *Star/Tribune* would emulate the action of the *St. Paul Pioneer Press* and *Dispatch* and drop all sauna, etc., advertising. Maybe it will spur some kind of activity by our City Council on how such places are licensed.

As ever,

* * * *

January 23, 1979

Maybe it is "beating a dead horse." Maybe it is old hat. Maybe a Rabbi, or a Priest, or a Minister, or all three together do not have sufficient power to bring adequate pressure. Maybe there is nothing anyone can do. But I must keep trying.

It's those "sauna, rap parlor, massage parlor, hostess service ads" in the *Minneapolis Star and Tribune*, once again.

When we protested over a year ago and were "double-talked" about freedom of press, we were disappointed. We felt that our intelligence had been insulted and that this was another instance of the profit principle overriding or undermining community concern. "If a business is licensed by the city," the paper's publisher told us in effect, "we are committed to accept its advertisement." Even though we knew and pointed out that the outstanding newspapers in the country do not follow that procedure, I and my protesting colleagues got nowhere. We took our licks and shrugged the matter off as a lost cause.

Well, the other day I was in one of our leading hotels and at every washbowl in the men's room was a printed message advertising "superb anatomical manipulation at your discretion," "aesthetically pleasing models," "open every day, 24 hours," etc. It was from one of the *Star and Tribune's* daily clients.

A hotel has no control over the distribution of such material. But the newspaper — though its wording is more discreet — does. And its advertisements are not limited to men's rooms. They get into our homes.

Rather than hiding behind the "freedom of press" and "city license" excuses and exploiting the sauna enterprise for gain, the *Star and Tribune* should take another look at its purpose and role in our town. Soliciting, in any guise, is not one of them.

As ever,

Dr. Yaacov Yankelevich

July 6, 1976

I mentioned Dr. Yaacov Yankelevich in my sermon, "Thanksgiving or Gratefulness." I did not mention him when I wrote this message a year and a half earlier. He is presently a practicing physician in our area and is a contributing member of Temple and our community. My helping him is among the best things I have ever done.

There is one phase of Dr. Yankelevich's story that I have not revealed before but which you may find interesting and even distressing.

When Dr. Yankelevich first came to see me, I immediately thought of going to the Federation. Here was a man anxious to pursue his profession (he was then working as a scrub nurse at Mt. Sinai Hospital), who could not be retrained for any other work and who could become a most productive member of our society. What an opportunity for Federation to establish some kind of loan fund for men and women in similar predicaments. It would be the "Jewish" thing to do — for our tradition tells us that the highest form of "tsedakah" is to see to it that the recipient never has to seek "tsedakah" again.

I met with the president of the Federation and made the suggestion to him. He would hear nothing of it. He did not even offer to take the idea to his Executive Committee or to his Board. And I pursued it no further with him.

Incidentally, when Dr. Yankelevich received his license to practice, he sent me a card on which he wrote, "Thank you, Rabbi Shapiro, for recreating me." It brought tears to my eyes. I don't know if "recreating" was the word he wanted to use, but for me it was a moment of fulfillment. For doesn't the Talmud tell us that "if we save one life it is as if we had saved the entire world?" And in a most essential way, Dr. Yankelevich's life was saved.

* * * *

One of the rewards of being a rabbi is the opportunities we have to perform a mitzvah. I suspect that rabbis have more such opportunities than most of you. That is the nature of our being.

But, often the mitzvah is just that — an opportunity. We need help to accomplish it.

Many of you know that I have been concerned with the Russian immigrants who have come to our community. They are brought here through the Federation and provisions are made for their maintenance until they can manage. But needs beyond the necessary cannot be promised or provided — especially in the area of university education. There are no funds to send a Russian immigrant to college or to help a professional be retrained.

Recently the case of a 52-year-old physician with a wife and university-age son came to my attention. In Kiev he was a well-known obstetrician, but because of language difficulties and the differences in medical training, it was necessary for him to have some retraining before he could pass the licensing examinations. With the gift of a few physicians as the basis, I wrote to some forty men, inviting them to participate in the mitzvah of sending this doctor back to school for six months, so that he could become the productive and contributing member of our community that he should be. Their response was most gratifying, and we may soon reach our goal.

Today he is finishing his first month at the Medical School of the University of Miami, one of the two schools where such retraining is offered. In a few months he will be back to enter the final phase that will bring him into the mainstream of medical life.

And that is what I call a "mitzvah."

As ever,

Washington, D.C.

I think that I first became fascinated with American History in the eighth grade, but it was not until I was a senior at the Boston Public Latin School that a Mr. Pierce, our history teacher, intrigued me with the events leading to the Revolution, the people who fought in it and the men who devised the Declaration of Independence and the Constitution. I could not read enough, thereafter, about Alexander Hamilton and Thomas Jefferson who shaped so much of our early destiny.

Never did I dream then that a sermon of mine would appear in the "Congressional Record" or that I would have four "official" invitations to Washington. Never in my wildest imaginings could I conceive that I would be at the White House and be introduced to the President of the United States by the Vice President. Who would have thought then that I would give a prayer to open the Senate or that Bernice and I would be invited to the signing of a peace treaty between Israel and Egypt and to the State dinner that followed. "Only in America."

You may be interested to learn how and why Senator Humphrey placed my sermon in the Congressional Record.

As many of you know, I had been stationed in Cairo during World War II. My task was to write the history of the AACS (the Army Airforce Communications System) in the area, and because of that I had an opportunity to learn about U.S. bases in that part of the Middle East. One of those installations was at Sharjah in Saudi Arabia.

Sharjah was unbearably hot and barren, and our American personnel was rotated from there with precise regularity. No one stayed more than three or six months, as far as I can recollect, and everyone had to go there — that is, except the Jewish personnel. It wasn't that we were somehow special. It was that the Saudis would not permit anyone Jewish on their territory.

Though we continued to have military posts in Arabia after the war, that policy of discrimination continued, and our government continued to acquiesce. No one seemed to be doing anything about it. And so, after I became a rabbi, I decided to raise the issue publicly.

As part of my preparation, I conferred about some of the legal aspects of what I was to say with the late Roger Joseph, an attorney and friend. Roger sent the sermon to Senator Humphrey who wrote to me on June 1, 1956:

Dear Rabbi Shapiro,

Roger Joseph was good enough to send me your most excellent sermon on Saudi Arabia's discriminatory visa policies.

This subject has been raised frequently on the Senate floor lately, and I wanted to share your statement with my colleagues. Consequently, I took the liberty of inserting it in the Congressional Record on May 17, and I am attaching the appropriate excerpt for your files.

I look forward to seeing you sometime soon in Minneapolis. Best wishes.

Sincerely,

Hubert H. Humphrey

Here is the excerpt from the Congressional Record and two Rabbi's Messages I wrote after my visits to Washington.

* * * *

Discrimination by Saudi Arabia
Against Americans of Jewish Faith

Mr. Humphrey. Mr. President, three months ago on the Senate floor I raised the issue of discrimination by the Government of Saudi Arabia against Americans of Jewish faith. Since that time this issue has been receiving increased attention at home and abroad. On various occasions both President Eisenhower and Secretary Dulles have admitted and defended this Government's acquiescence in these discriminatory practices. I should like to repeat today my condemnation of an unalterable opposition to our official position on this matter.

Recently, Rabbi Max A. Shapiro, of Temple Israel in Minneapolis, Minn., delivered a lecture on this subject entitled "A Matter of Principle." I should like to commend that lecture to the attention of my colleagues. It is an accurate historical review of similar incidents in American history when nations with whom we had treaty obligations denied equal protection and equal privileges, under the law, to Americans of other religious faiths.

I am happy to note that in other instances, going back to the earliest days of this country, back to the days of President Buchanan, back to the early 1800's and 1900's, our Government has stood for principle, and has either abrogated a treaty, or has insisted that the laws of other nations be amended so that Americans could be treated on the basis of equity and equality.

This is a fundamental principle. Our Constitution provides that there shall be no discrimination on the basis of religious affiliation.

Mr. President, I think it is about time the Congress of the United States paid more attention to some of the executive agreements, and, indeed, some of the treaty obligations into which we have entered which permit the kind of religious discrimination and second-class citizenship for American citizens to which I have referred.

I ask unanimous consent that the lecture by Rabbi Shapiro be printed in the RECORD at this point in my remarks.

There being no objection, the lecture was ordered to be printed in the RECORD, as follows:

A Matter of Principle[1]
Aspects of United States Policy in the Middle East

It is not my purpose this evening to talk to you about the crisis in the Middle East, the effect of the new cease-fire agreement, or whether war is inevitable despite all that has occurred. All this you can obtain in the newspaper accounts and in magazines from sources far more authoritative than I.

What I do propose to consider is a matter of principle — a matter of principle relative to the relation of our country to Saudi Arabia.

On February 24th[2] Secretary of State Dulles appeared before the Senate Foreign Relations Committee. He was questioned on American policy in the Near East, and he made a number of remarks indicative of the attitude of the State Department — remarks which bear some scrutiny.

In answering questions about Arabia's discrimination against American Jews in particular and Jews in general, Mr. Dulles made the statement that there was animosity present because the Arabs credited the Jews with the assassination of Mohammed. Where or how he arrived at this conclusion I do not know, but that it was completely erroneous is most evident. For the Koran — the Holy Scripture of the Arab world — describes in great detail the natural death of Mohammed, and it is there for anyone to see. When Mr. Dulles learned of the factual inaccuracy of his testimony, he had the official record corrected, deleting the assertion that the Jews had killed Mohammed. The statement was made to read that Arab animosity goes back to the time of Mohammed, some 1300 years ago.

The State Department's Attitude

This attitude of justification of Arab discrimination against Jews evinced a number of protests from the American Jewish community, but it was a second statement made by Mr. Dulles to which I want to call your attention at this time.

On questioning by Senator Humphrey, the Secretary of State admitted that no Americans of Jewish faith have been assigned to service at Dahran, the United States Airbase in Saudi Arabia. This, he explained, was in pursuance of an executive agreement of 1951 — an agreement

[1] April, 1956
[2] 1956

which does not require congressional action. On further questioning he indicated that we as a nation tolerate such discrimination "in order that this country and the Arab states may get along together to mutual advantage." "We hope," he stated, "that there can be greater moderation and greater tolerance but we cannot prescribe it from abroad or expect to bring it about suddenly."

This raises some interesting and provocative questions. Are Americans who happen to be Jews placed in a second class category because of their religion? Is our government because of pressure from an outside source abrogating a basic principle of American democracy? Is our State Department more interested in expediency than principle? Are the rights of American citizens expendable items to be bargained away on the international trading counter?

Let us look at the record.

The Treaty with Switzerland

In 1851, the American minister to Switzerland signed a treaty with the Swiss Federation establishing the rights of the citizens of each country to travel and visit in the other. Specifically it stated that the citizens of both countries "shall be admitted and treated upon a footing of reciprocal equality." Now the Swiss Confederation consisted of a number of Cantons, each governed by its own constitution, some of which subjected the Jews to severe restrictions and disabilities; and when five years later in 1856, a Mr. A.H. Goodman, an American Jew, was threatened with expulsion from one of the Cantons, he appealed to Theodore Fay, the American minister. Mr. Fay found that under the provisions of the treaty, he was powerless to help.

But the case became known to the general American public. Jews in America held protest meetings. Editorial comments in the newspapers bolstered them. Christians everywhere came to their support. An American principle was at stake. A committee headed by Rabbi Isaac M. Wise, the outstanding leader of Reform Judaism, was dispatched to meet with President James Buchanan to protest. And the President promised to do his utmost to change the prevailing condition.

From the exchanges that followed between the two governments it was evident that the Swiss cantons would have to amend their basic laws if American Jews were to have the same rights as other Americans within their borders. The United States was adamant — President Lincoln even going so far as to appoint a Jew as consul to Zurich. In 1874 the Swiss Confederation adopted a new constitution which erased all distinction between religions.

The Russian Treaty

A similar situation developed in our relations with Russia during the 19th century.

In 1832 the United States concluded a treaty of commerce and navigation with Russia. This agreement specified that American citizens might enter and reside in that country subject to local laws and ordinances. As you know, the 1800's were years of vast Russian persecution against the Jews, and Russia, taking her stand on the proviso that Americans were subject to local laws and ordinances, asserted the right to subject American citizens of Jewish faith to the same restrictions that she imposed on her own Jewish subjects.

Nothing was done until 1866 when a specific incident arose. An American Jew, Theodore Rosenstraus by name, was denied the right to acquire real estate in the city of Kharkov simply because he was a Jew. His appeal for diplomatic aid, coupled with the appeal of another American Jew who was banished from St. Petersburg because of his religion, set off a series of diplomatic exchanges between the two countries.

The United States took the position that "it could not accept any construction of the existing treaty that discriminated against any class of American citizens on account of their religious faith." And although the Russians maneuvered and replied that "it was the desire of the Emperor to show all possible consideration to American citizens," new cases in the controversy continued to crop up. In 1893, the news that Russia was refusing to grant visas to American Jews precipitated resolutions in Congress calling upon the President to put an end to such religious discrimination.

Exchanges between the two governments continued. In 1907, however, our State Department issued a new note — a note that abdicated the American position to Russian demands. This pronouncement stated that all Americans who had been former Russian subjects could not expect American protection should they return to Russia for any purpose.

There was a vigorous ourcry of protest from the American Jewish Community. It demanded that the basic treaty of 1832 be revoked and that a new treaty be drafted — a treaty in which there would be no ambiguity as to the complete equality of American Jewish citizens.

Our Government's Attitude

Our government vacillated. It pointed out the importance of the Far Eastern trade with Russia. At a conference with representatives of the B'nai B'rith, the American Jewish Committee and the Union of American Hebrew Congregations, President Taft read a prepared paper to the effect that abrogation of the treaty would do more harm than good. It would not only hurt the country, he said, it could harm the Jews. Large investments in Russia would be jeopardized. Even war might ensue.

But the matter had now been taken up by the American public. It was a matter of principle not investments. The constitution not only proclaimed the equality of each citizen but demanded no distinction among citizens because of religion. How could the United States possibly maintain a treaty in which these principles were ignored by the other side?

Now the protests to the treaty on this matter of principle grew. A national citizens committee headed by two distinguished Americans,

Andrew D. White, a former Russian ambassador, and William D. McAdoo, a prominent lawyer, was formed to press the issue. State legislatures passed resolutions calling for termination of the treaty. The pressure mounted and mounted. Finally in 1911, the House of Representatives voted 300 to 1 that the treaty be annulled. Before the measure could reach the Senate, the United States government cancelled the agreement.

The Matter in Question

Which brings us to the matter in question.

What is the situation in regard to Saudi Arabia? We do not have a treaty in the general terms of the Swiss or Russian agreements. The only provision that bears upon our problem is the standard principle in international law whereby any state can exclude the nationals of any other state. We as a nation have the right, and we exercise that right, to scrutinize the credentials of all members of foreign missions who come to this country.

On the surface there is no breach when Americans unfavorable to the Arabian government are refused admittance — or when our government does not submit the names of such persons when it presents a list of the members of our military or diplomatic mission. There is no breach of international law, but for us Americans there is a moral breach. It is the same moral violation that existed in our confrontations with Switzerland and with Russia.

A lie is not necessarily verbal! Discrimination is not only an overt act! A lie can be told by silence. Discrimination can be practiced by innuendo, by a shrug, by a wink of the eye.

And in the case of our relations with Arabia, discrimination is being practiced by inference. I know Dahran, the Arabian air base. I was there in 1944. No American soldier cherishes duty in that heat and sand. But this is a matter of principle: American citizens, American Jews in American uniforms, are being placed in a second class category because of their religion! And our State Department condones it! Mr. Dulles is very open about that! "We hope the situation will change, but we cannot prescribe it from abroad!" are his very words.

We cannot dictate it, it is true! We cannot prescribe it, it is true! But we need not subscribe to it!

When we did not subscribe to a similar policy in the case of Switzerland, the policy was altered. When we did not consent to it in the case of Russia we terminated our agreement. Are we so changed today? Are we so devoid of principle today?

Despite Different Conditions

I know that conditions are different. I know that we are now engaged in a vast cold war. I know that we are concerned with investments, with making friends, with security.

But we are not merely a body of investors. We are not merely intent upon making friends. We are not merely a nation out to encircle and entrap Russia. We are a country of free men!

Our greatness is built on our freedom. Our freedom is moral not material. We, as a people, have a great passion for gain. We should have a deeper passion for the rights of man. The principles on which this country was founded and nurtured are not incompatible with great material prosperity. But we should be unwilling to have prosperity, we should be unwilling to have great gain, if citizens must be shunted for it — if they must lose the rights which belong to every American. The cost is far too high! The price is far too great!

* * * *

November 1, 1977

Over the years I have had the privilege of meeting and being with Presidents Eisenhower and Johnson, but one of my greatest thrills was being at the White House some days ago and meeting President Carter.

A group of us from Minnesota were invited to Washington, at our own expense, for a briefing on the Panama Canal treaties. Why we were chosen, I do not know — but off we went at 7:40 a.m. on October 12. We reached Washington at about 11:15 a.m. and cars were waiting to take us to the Senate Building for lunch with Senator Anderson. Then it was over to the White House to be with Vice President Mondale who had invited us for coffee.

We gathered in the Roosevelt Room at the White House. Coffee was available and we spent a few moments chatting and waiting. I happened to be standing at one of the doors when suddenly it opened, and in walked the Vice President. Behind him was President Carter.

Now I have known Vice President Mondale since he was the attorney general of our state, but I confess that the suddenness of his appearance with the President was startling. Because I was closest to the entrance, he saw me first and, taking the President by the arm, he guided him to me saying, "I want you to meet one of my dear friends, Rabbi Shapiro." I must tell you that I was virtually speechless.

Later we were briefed by the Vice President, Ellsworth Bunker, General Jones of the Joint Chiefs, members of the State and Defense Departments and finally by the President himself. He was as impressive as could be — knowledgeable, eloquent, logical, and persuasive. He answered every question directly and with ease, and he was with us for some 35 minutes. At 5:30 we were again on a plane and back in the city at 7:20 p.m.

I had been in favor of the treaties prior to the trip. The briefing assured me that I had been right.

As ever,

*   *   *   *

December 3, 1979

As you may know, I was privileged to give the invocation opening the United States Senate on November 13, and it was a thrill. I was ushered to the Senate by Senator Rudy Boschwitz and Senate Chaplain Edward Elson, and we stood at the entrance where Senator Dave Durenberger, Senator Robert Byrd and Senator Howard Baker were there to greet me.

At 10:30 a.m. a bell rang announcing the Senate was to begin its session. I was led to the podium by Senator Pryor of Arkansas who was to be the presiding officer for the morning and who introduced me. Then with Bernice watching from the "family" section of the Senate balcony, I gave the following prayer:

It is written —"And the Lord said, 'I will bless thee and make thy name great and be thou a blessing' " (Gen. XII: 2).

Heavenly Father, though often we do not express it, we thank You that we have been so richly blessed — blessed with a land of plenty; blessed with a heritage of freedom and justice; blessed with a people creative and purposeful.

We thank You that our name has been made great — that ours is a haven that many seek; that ours is a hope to which many aspire; that ours is a strength for which others wish.

And we pray that this land of ours may ever prosper and that it will always be a blessing — a home for the homeless; a champion for righteousness; a defender of humaneness and liberty; and that somehow through us there will emerge a world untroubled by war; unvexed by fear; untrammeled by hunger; unfettered by cruelty; a world where justice and freedom, compassion and opportunity will always prevail. May it be so, O Lord. Amen.

As Ever,

More Messages

Here are a few of the other "Messages" that I thought may be of interest to you.

*The first became the subject of an article in the **Minneapolis Star** and was later reprinted in the **Catholic Bulletin**. Each of the others stimulated many of you to drop me a note in appreciation.*

* * * *

December 13, 1977

I do not know the kind of instruction nurses receive at the various schools of nursing or the information imparted to nurse's aides and other personnel at the hospitals and nursing homes in our area, and frankly, I have not checked. But something about them has been bothering me for some time.

It is not what I see but what I hear that distresses me as I visit patients or residents. Hospital and nursing home personnel almost always refer to the patients and residents by their first names. And I think that is wrong.

I know that the personnel are attempting to make the patient or resident comfortable. I know that in many cases a long-term relationship has been developed between them. I know that the prime focus is a concern for the patient and the resident. And it may be that I am overly sensitive.

But it seems to me that if a physician has been accustomed to being called "doctor" throughout his productive career, then he should still be addressed as "doctor" in a nursing home. If a woman has been accustomed to being called "Mrs." by all except her close friends; if a man was known as "Mr." in his work and activities; then they deserve that courtesy when they are hospitalized or residents. There is much in hospitals and nursing homes that dehumanizes. Let us not consciously add to it.

Our Jewish tradition tells us to respect our elders. Is it not a matter of respect to address them in a way they consider proper? In the long run it is they whom we want to please.

As ever,

* * * *

May 18, 1976

Some days ago we received a placard at Temple which we were

144

asked to post. I don't know who brought it in, but it was an announcement of a lecture on a subject of Jewish interest.

This is how the announcement began: "The Jewish Community cordially invites you . . ." I am not sure how others reacted, but to me it was a prime display of "chutzpa."

There is a Jewish community, of course, but who makes up that community or who speaks for it is a matter of argument, speculation or subjective decision. Is it all the Jews who live in a given geographic area? Is it only those who identify with a Jewish institution? Is it the people who comprise the Board of the Federation? Is it the combined membership of the synagogues? Are the secular Jews included? What about students?

I have been invited to many things by a host of Jewish organizations — Hillel, the J.C.C., the Lubavitsch House, the Talmud Torah, JCRC-ADL, The Council of Jewish Women, Mt. Sinai Hospital, B'nai B'rith, Brandeis, ORT, etc., but never before by an anonymous group — or individual — that calls itself "The Jewish Community." Who authorized whom? Or is it just a name to use as one pleases?

The lecture that was advertised was most worthwhile, but the thoughtlessness — or the effrontery — of the publicity was an offense. I have no idea to whom to protest. Perhaps this will suffice.

As ever,

* * * *

February 12, 1974

Just about a year ago, the Supreme Court handed down its landmark decision providing for legal and safe abortions. The decision was the culmination of many years of struggle by groups and individuals who felt that the laws prior to that time had been discriminatory, unrealistic and harsh — that many unwanted children had been born, the poor had suffered most, and that illegal abortions abounded, often resulting in disease and death.

As you know, the court's action was not accepted in many quarters and a concerted and continuous effort was launched against it. Great pressure has been brought on Senators and Congressmen to support legislation contravening the ruling; and eighteen amendments have already been proposed to change the decision. The struggle to legalize abortion is not yet over.

Some years ago I testified before our own State Legislative Committee urging that Minnesota's then archaic abortion law be changed. I voted whole-heartedly at the 1969 Biennial Convention of the Union of American Hebrew Congregations for the resolution favoring legalized abortion — a resolution which passed overwhelmingly. I applauded the Supreme Court decision when it was made and I still applaud it.

I hope you will join me in every effort to see that the Court's decision is not altered.

As ever,

* * * *

January 18, 1972

December has gone and with it the tensions, the discomfort, the concerns that touch so many of us who have children in school.

Some two months ago the St. Louis Park School System issued "guidelines" for its teachers as the Christmas season approached. They were based on "guidelines" prepared by the State Board of Education and were, after some controversy, put into effect in the schools.

I do not want to discuss the "guidelines" or my reactions to them here. Nor do I want to discuss the School Board meeting in St. Louis Park after their promulgation, or the means the School Board has selected for resolving the dilemma in the future. I want to comment, just briefly, on an editorial in the *St. Louis Park Sun* pertaining to the issue, and hopefully to clarify an essential point.

The editor presents, with honest feeling and clarity, a well-meaning solution. He advocates teaching about Judaism and Christianity in the schools and observing their religious holidays when they occur.

Unfortunately he is confused about the law governing such cases, the basic American principle of separation of church and state, and the sensibilities and rights of the individuals who attend our public schools.

It is permissible for schools to teach about religion, and I hope your children learn not only about the religions of the Western world but also about the East and about Humanism and Atheism too, for they will have to know and comprehend Russian and Chinese thinking. I do not know who is competent to teach Judaism, Christianity, Islam, Buddhism, etc., in our schools, but that is another matter.

It seems to me, however, that the editor should know that what he suggests is not only contrary to the law, but that there is an unbridgeable difference between learning about and understanding the history, customs, and tenets of a religion and being compelled indirectly or directly, into religious observance. The former is educational and enlightening and can lead to good will. The latter is divisive and demeaning — demeaning not only to the self-image of the individual who feels he must conform, but also to the "compeller" who places himself in the role of benevolent intimidator.

As ever,

* * * *

February 27, 1973

I need not tell you that death is no stranger to me. I see it far too often. I try, as best I can, to bring some comfort, some strength, some understanding to the bereaved, as you do too. But as the days pass we each go our respective ways. We have our own families, our work, our homes, our day-to-day activities. And for those who have most acutely suffered the loss that death brings, loneliness sets in.

I try my very best to keep in touch with them. But that certainly is not enough. How many of you, their friends, have picked up the phone just to call — if nothing more. Don't expect them to call you. Their lives have changed. They may be apprehensive about a new kind of relationship. They do not want to impose themselves upon you. It is for you to make the gesture, for you to reach out — you who are so much more fortunate, whose husband or wife is still with you.

And to a lesser degree, the same is true with divorce.

Sometime ago, a friend of mine — a clergyman — went through that experience. When I heard the news I was surprised and sorry, but I did nothing. Then one day we happened to meet.

"You know," he said to me, "not one of my friends called me when I was divorced. No one said a word."

"But what was there to say?" I asked. "We all knew you both, we all were your friends. What was there to say?"

"It isn't what you could say," he countered. "All you had to do

147

was call. All you had to do was say 'I hope everything is all right. Is there anything I can do?' We who are hurt want to know our friends are still there."

As ever,

* * * *

March 15, 1977

I enjoy travel. I like getting up early in the morning to catch an early plane for wherever my destination may be.

But I am affronted on some of those morning flights. It may be 6:00 a.m., 7:00 a.m., 8:00 a.m. As soon as the plane is in the air, there is the liquor cart. Before breakfast is served it is rolled down the aisle. "Have your morning whiskey!" And people do. I don't know whether it is their habit at home; because they are on a plane; or simply because airplane drinking is relatively inexpensive. But that is how some flights begin.

Then, on a recent trip, there was the free champagne. Over and over again, the cart made its excursion down the aisle. Plastic glasses clinked all the way from Minnesota to California.

I am not a teetotaler. Drinking does not offend me. But while we are looking — some of us — at the deteriorating of our society — the violence, the pornography, the corruption, etc. — let's take a look at this airline custom and policy.

Is it necessary to serve liquor in flight? Is it necessary for our health and our enjoyment? Do we need it to stimulate conversation or allay our fear of heights? And who knows, maybe the cost of air travel would be less expensive if all that champagne were kept in some closet.

As ever,

* * * *

April 23, 1972

I am letting my hair grow long, and the reactions have been many.

As yet there has not been any audible gasps when I face the Ark and the Congregation sees the back of my head, but at the Oneg Shabbats following, the comments go something like this: "Rabbi, don't cut your hair, I like it;" or "Rabbi, (and this with an understanding smile) — you look just like a hippy;" or "Have you lost some weight, Rabbi? You seem different;" or "Rabbi, you look so young these days."

But nothing matches my experience at one of the hospitals the other day. The lady I was about to visit was in excruciating pain. While recovering from a very serious illness, she had accidentally fallen and shattered a hip, and the shock of the fall had brought on even further suffering and complications.

I walked into her room. The tubes and intravenous bottles seemed to engulf her. Her eyes were closed, but I could see the tears and I could hear the quiet sobs. Her husband stood by, his face steeped in sympathetic pain. I nodded to him, and to her I said, "Hello _____, it's Rabbi Shapiro."

She opened her eyes slowly and looked at me. Then she raised her head just a bit to get a clear glimpse. The sobs stopped, so did the tears. "Rabbi," she said, and her voice became full and strong. "Rabbi, you're letting your hair grow too long." With that, her head fell back on the pillow, her eyes closed again, and the tears began to flow once more.

I am letting my hair grow long. And there have been all kinds of reactions.

As ever,

* * * *

Sunday, October 10, 1971

This day began like so many others.

The morning sky was a perfect Minnesota blue, when I looked out my study window. Leaves dotted the lawns everywhere. The trees were in their brightest autumn finery. "Thank You, God," I said. "Thank You for this magnificent day."

I could hear the coffee perking downstairs — and Bernice. I thought of Steven, whom we would see later that afternoon, and Susan, busy in London. All well. All happy. "Thank You, God," I said. "Thank You for those I love."

I drove along Lake of the Isles to the Temple. The air was clear. The water calm. The breeze refreshing. "Thank You, God," I said. "Thank You for beauty everywhere."

There was a fire-drill at Temple when I got there. The kids came down the stairs, hurrying to get outside. "Hi, Rabbi," they called. Or they waved and smiled. "Thank You, God," I said.

149

"Thank You for work that brings me joy."

In the afternoon, Bernice and Steve and I were at the rally for Soviet Jewry and we heard the urgent plea of Professor Mikhail Zand.* "Thank You, God," I said. "Thank You for the human spirit. Thank You for the opportunity to help. Thank You for the freedom in our own blessed land."

Later we called on Cantor Katz who had just been bereaved, and he and I talked for some time. "Thank You, God," I said. Thank You for the strength to overcome adversity."

And then in the evening there was a Service. Shemini Atzeret. Coming to a close was Succot, our Festival of Thanksgiving. And again I said, "Thank You, God. Thank You," this time because our tradition prescribes it.

But then, isn't almost every moment of our lives a time to give thanks?

As ever,

---

*Professor Mikhail Zand was a recent immigrant from the U.S.S.R. He spoke at the University of Minnesota.

In Retrospect

As I was writing the introduction to this compilation of sermons and Rabbi's Messages, it occurred to me that, in some measure, I was putting together a personal history of the last quarter of a century of Temple life.

That being the case, I have added a few "notes" and a list of some of the major happenings at Temple over the past few years. These you will find at the end of the volume.

And then I thought I would enumerate for you some of the innovations that have taken place in the seventeen years that I have been the Senior Rabbi at Temple. Sometimes the changes were imperceptible as when the rabbis put on the tallit for Shabbat Services. We had worn them only on the High Holy Days and at Confirmation prior to that. Sometimes they seemed startling as when women held the Torahs before the entire congregation while the Cantor chanted the Kol Nidre on Yom Kippur eve. Actually, some changes were made in almost every facet of our congregational worship and program.

Our Sabbath Services

Let us begin with our Sabbath Services and the liturgy we use for them. Most of you recall Union Prayer Book I. For its time it was a remarkable achievement, and we used it every Friday evening and Saturday morning with great satisfaction. There was much about it that I prefer to "Gates of Prayer" which we use, in part, these Shabbat eves.

Union Prayer Book II also served us remarkably well, but both volumes were obviously dated. They had been compiled before the occurrence of the two most monumental events in Jewish history in the last 1900 years: the Holocaust and the rebirth of the State of Israel.

There was a distinct need for prayerbooks that were less archaic in language and more pertinent in meaning. I knew that a Committee of the Central Conference of American Rabbis was at work on such a project, but I was not certain when it would be completed. And I did not want to wait or resort to "Creative Services" more and more.

Those were the conditions that led to the development of our "Supplementary Service for the Sabbath" and then to the Supplement to our High Holy Day Services, both of which you approved immediately and which added a new and contemporary spirit to our worship. At approximately the same time, I compiled a Selichot Service[1], and not too long thereafter I put together our special "Service for the House of Mourning" and a "Daily Worship Service." These[2] not only replaced the Services from Union Prayer Book I, but they provided a new dimension to the Shiva and Daily Worship.

"Gates of Prayer" and "Gates of Repentance," the new Holy Day Prayerbook, are now our "official" Reform Prayerbooks. As you know, we use them, with modifications, for our Services, but we also continue to use our Supplements. The combination has been most effective.

---

[1]We instituted Selichot Services in 1961 and held them in the Deinard Chapel. In 1963 we moved into the Sanctuary, not merely to accommodate the growing numbers of people who attended, but also to add the voices of the choir to the Service.

[2]The "Service for the House of Mourning" and the "Daily Worship Service."

Other Innovations

There were other innovations for the Sabbath. In 1965 we began to read from the Torah every Friday evening. That was the result of one of our Men's Club Retreats which Gerry Robbins used to arrange.

At one of our sessions at the Retreat we were discussing "Prayer and Worship" and that led to my asking the men, "How can we make our Sabbath Services more meaningful?" Among the suggestions was, "Why not read the Torah on Friday evenings?" As you undoubtedly know, many Reform congregations were already doing this, and we had also on special occasions. From that time on, however, I made it a regular component of our Shabbat eve worship. Not only has this practice enhanced our Service, but it has provided us with an additional opportunity to involve congregants in it. Each Friday eve we invite two members of the congregation to participate in the Torah Service and to recite the blessings before and after the reading.

Confirmation and Bar/Bat Mitzvah

One of the essential tenets of Reform Judaism is that it can change to meet changing conditions and needs. The early "reformers," almost 200 years ago, determined that women should be the equal of men in the synagogue, and that girls, therefore, should have the same religious education as boys. They could not then conceive of Bat Mitzvah, but they were right in concluding that a Hebrew education in itself was not a Jewish education. So they developed the concept of Confirmation for Jewish life where young men and women would receive the same schooling and affirm their faith in the same way and at the same time.

As in many Reform congregations, Bar Mitzvah was not an integral part of our Temple program prior to 1955. We did not have our own Hebrew School until 1954, and though there had been an occasional Bar Mitzvah before then, training generally had to be done elsewhere. Bat Mitzvah was not permitted under any circumstances.

In most Orthodox and Conservative congregations throughout the country, a Bar Mitzvah signaled the end of that young man's religious education. For girls there was relatively little. Few went to Hebrew School, and even after 1922 when the first Bat Mitzvah took place, there was no rush to initiate that ceremony.

Importance of Confirmation

It is easy to understand, then, why Confirmation was so important in Reform Judaism. It occurred at the end of the tenth grade, usually sixteen years of age, rather than the thirteen of Bar Mitzvah. It was a more fitting age for the culmination of one's Jewish education and the affirmation of one's faith. It was not dependent merely on some knowledge of Hebrew but on a graduated educational program. Girls were included, the rabbis were most often the teachers, and the Confirmation ceremony was beautiful and meaningful. It was no wonder that the Confirmands looked forward to it, and the social events that followed, with abounding excitement and enthusiasm.

Gradually, however, Bar Mitzvah began to be part of our Saturday Morning Service at Temple. In 1955, the Bar Mitzvah took place at the time of our Jr. High School Saturday Service. Evelyn Segal, as some of you may recall, was our organist for that Service; we used the old "Union Hymnal" for our liturgy; and there was no Cantor or choir.

Change on Saturday Morning

Among the first things I did when I became the Rabbi of the Temple was to enhance the Saturday Morning Service with cantor and choir (the Religious School had already begun to have its own Service earlier in the morning), to deepen and augment the Hebrew training, and to institute Bat Mitzvah. The latter was no easy matter, for though it seemed to me — as it did to the majority of our Temple Task Force that studied it — that if women were to be equal to men in Reform Judaism, Bat Mitzvah had to be available to them, there was much opposition. Incidentally, the oldest person to be a Bat Mitzvah at Temple was Raleigh Liebenberg. The ceremony took place in 1977 when she was 84 years old.

As most of the boys at Temple began to be Bar Mitzvah and as approximately half of the girls were being Bat Mitzvah, there was a challenge to Confirmation. Even though every Bar/Bat Mitzvah — with one or two annual exceptions — stayed with us through Confirmation, so many had experienced the exhilaration of Bar/Bat Mitzvah and the social excitement that followed, that there was the danger that Confirmation might be secondary in their lives. We wanted them both to be life cycle ceremonies that they would always remember.

Ninth Grade Retreats

And so, we began to make changes in our Confirmation class program. The Temple Camp gave us one such opportunity, and we developed our ninth grade retreats. They began slowly under the direction of Robert Fisher, who had been our Bar/Bat Mitzvah Director from 1967 to 1974 and were brought to their present superb status by Rabbi Barack who came to Temple in 1973 and Rabbi Zemel who came in 1979. The Confirmation Class began to write its own Confirmation Service (the rabbis had written it prior to 1970) and to participate in singing part of the Service. We developed the Confirmation poster,* changed the class structure and, thank God, Confirmation still is a viable and vital part of our Temple activities.

Meanwhile our Bar/Bat Mitzvah program began to play a meaningful role in the lives of the Bar/Bat Mitzvah and their families. In many ways it was a response to the program and Service we had created, for though our emphasis was on Hebrew training it was also focused on helping our young people mature and to think through his/her relationship to family, to Jewish life and the future.

Chanting The Kiddush

Although parents had asked again and again that we permit their Bar/Bat Mitzvah to chant the Kiddush, or to read part of the Service or to have the Bar/Bat Mitzvah on Friday evening, I had resisted. Some youngsters can chant the Kiddush beautifully; others cannot. Some youngsters read Hebrew and English well; others have difficulty. In some congregations where the Bar/Bat Mitzvah is part of the Shabbat Evening Service, the Service can

---

*The Confirmation poster is the result of a competition for the Design Class at the Minneapolis School of Art and Design. The posters that have been created are displayed for the Confirmation Class which makes the selection. The selected poster is then reproduced and each Confirmand receives a copy. Posters can be seen in the Youth Lounge.

not only become unconscionably long, but the Bar/Bat Mitzvah tends to become a focal point. In time, those who wish to attend for worship, for intellectual or spiritual stimulation, for the aesthetics of the Service, may begin to stay away.

This, it seemed to me, could well have happened to us, for our Bar/Bat Mitzvah Service is designed to be a personal one. It centers on the boy or girl. The talk is directed to them. Their parents have an opportunity to speak to them. It is family oriented, stressing the relationship of the Bar/Bat Mitzvah to parents and siblings. It is not merely meant to display a skill in chanting or reading Hebrew, but to indicate that the Bar/Bat Mitzvah has given deep thought to their hopes, their dreams, their concern for Judaism and Jewish life. I did not want to destroy that.

Family Participation

Of course, there was some family participation on Friday evenings. We did ask the mother of the Bar/Bat Mitzvah to say the blessing over the Sabbath candles. Sometimes a sister or grandmother joined with her. I prepared a booklet of prayers for them from which to choose, or they were at liberty to write their own prayer. Sometimes if siblings had been Bar/Bat Mitzvah in previous years, they participated in the Friday evening Torah Service. But it was only after I had compiled our "Supplementary Service for the Sabbath" and had included an English introduction to the Kiddush appropriate for a Bar/Bat Mitzvah to read, that the boy or girl participated.

I must confess that took some prodding. Too often one becomes so inured to custom and tradition that a change for the better just can't be perceived. It takes another eye to see it, a different heart to feel it, a fresh intellect to understand it. For too long the Bar/Bat Mitzvah had not participated on Friday evenings because there was no place in our Service. Even after there was a place — the Supplementary Service — we continued with the old and tried custom. But one day, before her son was to be a Bar Mitzvah, Natalie Fischman came to see me about the matter and gave me the stimulus and opportunity to rethink it. Now it is our custom for the Bar/Bat Mitzvah to read the introduction to the Kiddush and to join with the Cantor in leading the entire congregation in chanting it — and I am grateful to Nat.

The High Holy Days

As the congregation continued to grow, the High Holy Days presented a problem for us. The two consecutive evening Services and the two morning Services which had become standard by 1963 were no longer adequate for our numbers. There were three choices. We could divide the congregation and hold simultaneous Services in Minda and Joseph Halls as well as in the Sanctuary. We could go to some large auditorium that could seat the entire congregation at one time. Or we could attempt three consecutive Services in the evening and some other kind of adjustment for the morning Services. All of us on our Temple Board of Trustees were reluctant to leave the Sanctuary on Rosh Hashanah and Yom Kippur. To us it would have been an unseemly act. We wanted to remain in the Temple. Our sanctuary is too beautiful to be abandoned at our holiest time of the year. Moreover, our Board reasoned that identical Services in Minda and Joseph Halls, no matter how fair we might be in allocating places, would certainly make a goodly number of our congregants unhappy.

Though it would be a burden for the rabbis and though the Board did not want to urge it, I suggested that we try three consecutive Services on the High Holy Day eves, and it has been a boon for us. The Services are identical in every way, though we on the pulpit and in the choir may show some weariness during the last Service. And though there may be an occasional discontent because some of you must come at a time you did not request, it has gone amazingly well. We have much for which to thank Walter Baron and his staff; and Marvin Kahner and his ushers.

To ease the burden for the morning Services, I suggested a Creative Service, prepared and conducted by our Youth Group. Bob Fisher, our Bar/Bat Mitzvah Director, took it on as his task. The Services were initially held in Juster Auditorium and the Ben Friedman room, simultaneously with the two successive morning Services in the Sanctuary. They were an immediate success. In two years the attendance — youngsters, families, adults — outgrew the Religious School Building, and the Service was moved to Minda and Joseph Halls where we could seat more than 500 people. In the past years, under the supervision of Rabbi Barack and our Youth Directors and now with the presence of Rabbi

Zemel, the morning Creative Services have become an exciting and meaningful addition to our High Holy Day Worship.

The Yom Kippur Appeal

Every Yom Kippur Eve for as far back as anyone can remember, there was an appeal from the pulpit for support of our national institutions of Reform Judaism, the Hebrew Union College-Jewish Institute of Religion, and the Union of American Hebrew Congregations. Though it was an absolutely necessary budget requirement, it was for me and for many of you, I am sure, a jarring intrusion into the solemnity of our Service and somehow unsuitable for Kol Nidre eve.

I had wanted to eliminate the appeal from the moment I became the rabbi, but you responded so generously each year, I hesitated to make the suggestion to our Board. How could we destroy a process that had served us so well for so many years and for which there was no overt criticism!

In the last year of Sidney Cohen's presidency he approved a plan to do away with the evening appeal, and to initiate some other means of raising the funds. But I still dragged my feet. With inflation upon us, and budget problems in the offing, I was fearful of propelling our financial difficulties into a crisis. Suppose it did not work?

However, this past year (1979), with the firm support of Elliot Kaplan, our Temple president, and with the encouragement of the Board, we took the plunge. Instead of our annual verbal appeal, we asked you to make your Yom Kippur pledge via the mail. You were even more generous than when I made the appeal from the pulpit and our Yom Kippur Service will no longer be interrupted by a plea for funds.

Women In Our Servce

I suppose the most startling change in our High Holy Day Services was in 1965. That was when we began to invite the women of the congregation to participate in the Torah Service of those two days. Many eyes were raised, but it was accepted as natural. Even more startling was our Yom Kippur evening Service of 1979. It was the first time that women of our Temple stood before the congregation and held the Torahs while the cantor and choir chanted the Kol Nidre. I had hesitated with this innovation, not because I thought the congregation would be offended, but because I did not know how women would fare holding Torahs for some fifteen minutes. They did as well as the men.

The Three Festivals

Changes also were introduced into the Services for the three Festivals. In the past, our major Festival Service had been in the morning of the first and last days of Passover and Sukkot. Shavuot, of course, is the time of Confirmation, and that Service has a different tradition at Temple, one which we have retained. But for Passover and Sukkot, we began to observe our important Service in the evening. This not only gave more adults the opportunity to attend, but occasionally there is a Bar or Bat Mitzvah on those evenings. And we added a Yizkor Service.

Confirmation has remained the essence of our Service of Shavuot morning. Elsewhere I have enumerated some of the new approaches we took to it in our efforts to maintain the meaning and vitality it has had over the years.

There was also another change in our effort to bring additional meaning to the Festivals. As you know, Reform has been the great innovator in American Jewish religious life. About half a century ago it introduced the idea of Consecration, a Service for the young children recently enrolled in our Religious Schools. It is a time for families to come together to witness a blessing for their children and grandchildren, and to watch them receive a miniature Torah, symbolic of the educational experience that will be theirs. In most congregations, the Consecration Service is held in conjunction with Shemini Atzeret/Simchat Torah, the last day of Sukkot. The natural result has been that the celebration of Simchat Torah became exclusive for the Consecrants and their families.

Some years ago I separated the two. Simchat Torah is now a congregational Service which the entire congregation may enjoy, and Consecration takes place on an appropriate Sunday afternoon when the new children of our school, their families and friends can be together for this meaningful and joyful ceremony.

The Congregational Seder

I do not know whether Temple ever had a congregational Seder, but from the time I came to Minneapolis, and I assume for many years before that, there was none. The reasons were, and are, very valid. The place for a Seder is in the home.

In the last few years, however, I began to receive many requests from couples whose children were no longer in the city or from single parents who have no family in the area. And so we decided to try. Our first attempt in 1977 was also an immediate success, and the Congregational Seder on the second evening of Passover is now a happy fixture in our Temple life.

The Temple Camp

The purchase of the Temple Camp was an achievement I shall never forget. I remember sitting in the living room of Gerry Friedell's home in the summer of 1963. With us were Joe Kahn, our administrator in those days, Larry Greenberg, Dr. Sid Esensten, Buddy Rose, Dr. Norman Bloom, Saul Smiley, the late Dr. Jack Berg, and Babe Golden. Gerry had just become President of our Men's Club, and he was searching for a project that would ignite the men and simultaneously be of inestimable service to the congregation.

Our congregation has always been progressive. In 1947, under the direction of Rabbi Richard Singer, who was then the Associate Rabbi, a day camp was begun. It may have been the first such in the Twin Cities.

Camp Teko

In those early days, the youngsters were picked up by bus and taken to Lake Nokomis where the city had provided Temple with beach and beach house facilities for the morning. Then the campers were bussed to Temple for a hot meal and spent the afternoon in activities in our building and environs. At 3:00 p.m. or thereabouts they were bussed home. The camp, whose name was Camp Teko — "Te" for Temple, "Ko" for Nokomis — had a six week session. It was an excellent Day Camp, and Temple was justifiably proud of it.

When I came to Minneapolis in 1955, the Camp was under the direction of Harry Glasser, our Religious School Director. The basic change that had been made was the elimination of the hot lunch. The campers "brown bagged" it. The camp was still the best of its kind in the area. It still served only those youngsters ages five through nine, and it still was an outstanding part of our youth program.

Meanwhile other Day Camps had come into being with more suitable sites for camping; and the city had informed us that Lake Nokomis would soon no longer be available to us. We were at the point of either losing a most successful program or making accomodations that would not truly fit the needs of our Temple families.

I had hoped that we could acquire a campsite of our own, but the prospect of finding one within our means and close enough to where our people lived to make "bussing" feasible did not seem possible. Gerry, however, was fired by the idea, and he would not be deterred. His proposal to the group who met at his house was that the Men's Club purchase a site and then maintain it as an annual project. Everyone present responded with enthusiasm. A campsite, not only for Camp Teko but for other Temple programs, was a natural.

The Search for a New Site

Bud Rose was given the task of finding the proper place for us. Whether he discovered the present location or whether it was in conjunction with Gerry, I do not know. But with a proposal put together by Gerry and his group, coupled with an architectural design by Saul Smiley and aided by the financial backing of Sam Shapiro, the Men's Club purchased the former Boy Scout Camp Tonkawa, 18½ acres on Lake Minnetonka with enough facilities to have Camp Teko there immediately. And Art Jaffee, who was then chairman of our Camp Committee, saw to that.

That was the beginning, and it was not easy. Our Board of Trustees had to be assured that the camp would not be a burden on the Temple budget and that it would serve a useful congregational purpose. Repairs had to be made at the site; a beach had to be developed, a wharf installed. And this small group of dedicated men, with the consent and assistance of the Men's Club, did it. The camp was established as a Men's Club project, with a Men's Club commitment to maintain it financially. These men and the Men's Club Board not only made substantial contributions themselves, but they raised the funds, (the $80,000 purchase price had to be obtained through solicitation), they did the repairs, they made the facilities ready for occupancy.

Religious School Retreats

Within a year we began to use the camp for our Religious School as well. We devised weekend retreats and all day sessions. We tried a camp day for our college students. The Men's Club developed a picnic carnival on the ground, and during the summer months we held Friday evening Services simultaneous with those at Temple, for we had built an outdoor chapel on a ridge overlooking the lake.

In time our innovative Ninth Grade Retreat Program, retreats for the Youth Groups, Confirmation and Bar/Bat Mitzvah classes, and the individual camp days set aside for our other classes made the camp an integral part of our Religious School. We also experienced a weekend of Family Camping and looked forward to the time when there would be facilities adequate for expanding such activities.

Meanwhile our Summer Camp took on new dimensions. Other men and women began to be involved. We lengthened the Day Camp to nine weeks, began an overnight camp and developed leadership training programs for our teenagers. Confirmation and older high schoolers pitched in as Junior Staff for our retreats, and Jewish content began to supplement the camping skills and general enjoyment provided the campers.

A Jewish Camp

One of the reasons I had been so enthusiastic about acquiring a campsite was the hope — and the possibility — that it could not only enhance the Camp Teko program and serve our congregation in other ways, but that it would deepen and expand our Religious Education efforts. I had never attended a Jewish camp as a youngster. My camping experience had been secular. But I knew what was happening at camps sponsored by the Union of American Hebrew Congregations and how Jewishly meaningful such camps could be.

In our first years at the site, we tried to infuse Jewish content into our camp program, but we had neither the personnel nor the means to accomplish what I knew could be done. Though our camp was remarkably successful, I felt the lack. It was only with the coming of Rabbi Barack and Rabbi Zemel to Temple that the change was made. Jewish content and spirit now pervades every aspect of it.

Our Schools

When I came to Temple, Harry Glasser was the Director of our Religious and Hebrew School as well as our Youth Activities Director. He had given shape to our basic Religious School structures, and it was under his guidance that our Hebrew School was begun in 1954 and our Nursery School in 1955.

In 1957 it was decided that the Temple desperately needed a full time Administrator. Our budget, however, could not manage an Associate Rabbi (to which I was elected in 1957) and an Educational Director as well. And so Joe Lipkin who was president of the Temple at that time asked me to be the Educational Director for, as he put it, "a limited time."

Directors of Education

With the help of some of our congregants, primarily Phil Dolinger, Sam Perlman and Curtis Krishef, we managed rather well. In 1963 when I became Senior Rabbi we selected Charles Marks, a Minneapolis public school teacher, to direct the schools. He was followed by Marshall Kaner who was then a principal of one of the public schools. When Marshall became a supervisor in the public school system, Rabbi Rutman took over the directorship of the schools assisted by Mansour Alyeshmerni, and for one year thereafter Mansour was our full time Director.

In 1974 Sidney Weisberg, a man of much experience in Jewish education, came to us. Sid stayed with us for two years, stabilizing a variety of new programs, and tightening a number of administrative procedures that had been allowed to lapse. Joanne Glosser, a graduate of the Hebrew Union College-Jewish Institute of Religion's School of Education in Los Angeles joined us in 1977. A proponent of confluent education and endowed with an impressive background, she brought new concepts and content to the Religious School, and with Yoel Levy, our Hebrew School Director, developed an innovative Hebrew Learning Center and strengthened our Hebrew School.

Educational Innovation

Over the years we had done much pioneering in our Religious School. Besides the Ninth Grade Retreat Program, we developed learning trips out of the city for our Bar/Bat Mitzvah classes and for the Confirmation Class. These were designed not merely to show our students Jewish life in another community and to meet their peers in those towns, but to provide them the opportunity to make new friends at home. You may not realize it, but at one point we had more than fifteen different schools represented in our Confirmation Class. Often some of its members scarcely knew one another. The Bar/Bat Mitzvah trip has usually been to Chicago; the Confirmands have gone to Chicago, Winnipeg and recently to see Jewish New York.

The Nursery School

Our Nursery School was opened in 1955 with Roz Bearman as our Director and with but a handful of children. Over the years it has grown to full capacity, has been one of the schools constantly recommended by the University of Minnesota, and has developed a number of unusual activities and programs.

All of our Directors have been superb. Ceil Rozman succeeded Roz Bearman, and in time she was followed by Dorothy Sipkins who had been a teacher both in our Religious School and in the Nursery School. Dorothy brought a fresh outlook to the School and served as our Director with innovation and dedication for seventeen years. She resigned in 1977, and Joanne Blindman, who had been Supervisor of our Primary Department and a teacher in our Nursery School, was appointed Director. Joanne added her special quality to the classes with a new devotion and instituted a Toddlers Program for the very young and their parents and an afternoon Kindergarten Enrichment Program for children who attend public kindergarten in the morning. Both programs gained instant success, recognition and praise.

The Singles

Long before "single parents" became part of our vocabulary, we began such a group at Temple. In 1965 I was asked by some of our members who had been divorced to try to establish some kind of activity for them within the Temple structure. So I called them together with Callman Rawley who was then head of Jewish Family Service and Dr. Marvin Sukov, a psychiatrist, to discuss what might be done. "Parents Without Partners" was already in existence on a national scale, and we investigated becoming part of that movement and participating in its activities and success. But we wanted to limit our "Parents" to Jewish parents for obvious reasons, and this was impossible under the "Parents Without Partners" charter. So we began our own group. Initially all its members were members of the Temple, but we soon discovered that to have a worthwhile program we would have to open our group to the entire community. In time "singles" were also admitted to the Single Parents who changed its name to "Twin City Singles." It still meets and serves a most important need.

Our Temple Tours to Israel

More and more as I think back over the years, I realize how much of our Temple activities are a result of ideas that have come from individuals in the congregation. Our Temple tours to Israel was one.

Sometime in 1963, Gerry Friedell who was President of the Men's Club and Dr. Burton Diamond, one of his chairmen, came to me with a thought that was most exciting. It may not have been new to congregations around the country, but it was new to me and to our community: the Rabbi should lead a Temple tour to Israel.

At the time it seemed farfetched to me, but the Men's Club pursued it as one of its projects, and sure enough a Men's Club sponsored tour to Israel and Europe left Minneapolis in April of 1964. We were away almost a month, and besides ten days in Israel we visited Italy, Switzerland, Austria, France, and England. It was exciting, meaningful, exhausting, and exhilarating.

Three years later, we began a program of a Temple tour to Israel, with a short side trip to a European capitol, almost annually. Each tour has been equally full of exhilaration, excitement, meaning, and exhaustion. And each trip brings the participants close together, develops new friendships and creates a greater awareness of our Jewishness and our ties to Israel and Jews everywhere.

The Sabbath Family Dinners

Though our congregation is relatively large, I have always tried to make our members feel that it was comparatively small. And I have attempted to do it in a number of ways. There are the anniversary greetings and blessings, the birthday cards for our youngsters, and the constant endeavor to know each individual by name. I can't recall how many times I have been told that my "memory is fantastic." It may be; but "remembering" also includes much effort.

One of the ways I thought that a feeling of "smallness" might be generated was through Sabbath Family Dinners. I suggested this to the Sisterhood and Men's Club in the fall of 1972 for one of their projects, and as always they reacted with eagerness and a willingness to make it work. Our first such dinner took place on Friday, January 17, 1973, and it was over-subscribed. Sabbath family dinners became a monthly activity between October and April from that time on.

The dinners take place in Joseph Auditorium which seats approximately 150 individuals, and are generally served family style. The atmosphere can best be described as "shabbasdig" with an explanation of the rituals, with singing and delight.

Because there are always a goodly number of children present, there is also a short Sabbath Service after the meal. This gives those who feel they cannot stay for our regular Service an opportunity for Sabbath worship before going home.

On occasion, when there has been a Friday evening Family Service, the Couples Club has undertaken the Sabbath Dinner as one of its activities. The first one, which took place on Chanukah of 1979, was so well attended that the dinner had to take place in both Joseph and Minda Halls. It was a beautiful "family affair," and more such dinners are contemplated.

The Library

A library is an essential part of any congregation, and we can be justifiably proud of our Isaac Kaufman Library which was established with the opening of our Temple building in 1928.

Our library contains more than 7000 volumes and is among the finest collection of Judaica in the area. Besides an extensive Reference Section, the library provides vertical files, teacher resources and audio visual materials. A children's library has been established (The Shirley Schleiff Greenberg Fund) as well as a section specializing in current novels devoted to Jewish subjects (The Robert Geltman Fund). Moreover, the library purchases subscriptions to forty magazines of Jewish and scholarly content and eight newspapers including the *London Jewish Chronicle*, the *Jerusalem Post*, and the *Boston Jewish Advocate*; and participates in the inter-library loan system. It is a very busy place.

Georgia Kalman who is an accredited librarian began her work in the Temple library in 1952. Over the years she has not only helped develop the library to its present status but has coordinated her activities with her position as Administrative Assistant to the Director of Religious Education.

* * * *

And so it goes. Though Temple seems very much the same as it was twenty-five years ago when I first came to it, it is vastly different. And that, I believe, is what has kept our congregation interesting and vital.

Always Something New

In a Jewish community as large as ours — small though it is in comparison to the great metropolitan areas — there is not one Jewish agency that can adequately serve the particular needs of the individuals or families that comprise our population. A Jewish Family Service, good as it may be, reaches only a minimal number of those who need its services. Hillel touches relatively few of the Jewish students on campus. The Jewish Community Center, in whatever city it may be, claims but a fraction of the people with its variety of programs. It is the same with other "umbrella" groups: the Talmud Torah, the Sholom Home, Vocational Services, "Kibbutz and Ride," etc. And Federations, rightfully concerned with budget and finances, find it difficult to even consider the support of more than one "agency" in any given area of service.

It is the synagogue, I believe, that can be a supplement to virtually every program "community agencies" provide. That is why we, at Temple, have instituted a range of activities, some emulated by Federation sponsored agencies; others similar to those already in existence. These programs do not compete with Jewish Family Service, the Community Center, etc. They answer the needs of completely different groups of people, many who would never use the facilities offered by the "community."

Our New Horizon group is one such effort. There was a "Golden Age" club in the community in 1975, but very few of our Temple membership of that age attended its excellent program. We, at Temple, were reaching our children, our teenagers, our young marrieds; we were always attempting something for our singles, but we were not directing any attention to those over 55. And it was a concern.

One day Marge Mandel, a former Sisterhood president and a member of our Board of Trustees, and I discussed the entire matter of service to our over 55's. Spurred by her enthusiasm and creativity, we attempted a program and it just blossomed. It grew beyond our original speculations, brought new members into the congregation and has become one of our vital affiliates.

The Beginning

This is how the New Horizons came to be. Sometime in July of 1975, Marge and I began to move ahead with her thought. We decided to invite a few individuals whom we felt would be interested and enlist their ideas and their support. On August 5 we met with Marian (Mrs. J.J.) Kaplan, Eddie Schwartz, Sylvia and Elmer Marks, Annette (Mrs. Sam) Cohen, Sophie and Ray I. Bart. Lois (Mrs. Arnold) Rose was there as a Sisterhood representative. They were all enthusiastic about the idea and the prospects and we began to make plans.

Marge and I volunteered to identify all the Temple members who were 55 and over and according to the design of the Executive Committee (as our small group now called itself), we asked the 120 individuals to come together for an evening. Sixty men and women responded. On September 28 we all met for coffee and to react to the plans of the Executive Committee. Enthusiasm was unanimous.

The Program

That was the beginning. The first program, three weeks later, was a trip by chartered bus to Orchestra Hall to hear the Jerusalem Symphony Orchestra. It was a major success. And the New Horizons was off and running.

Our New Horizons presently has some 150 members. It meets

monthly for a dinner and usually provides one or two other events during that time span. Before every dinner meeting the members come to the Deinard Chapel for Daily Worship.

They have gone as a group to hear the Minnesota Opera Company, to the Chanhassen Dinner Theatre, and to the University of Minnesota Arboretum. They have taken a two day bus trip to Dodgeville, Wisconsin. They have sponsored Purim and New Year's Eve parties, have listened to book reviews and discussions on Medicare, art and theatre. And its record of attendance at meetings has been universally and phenomenally high.

The success of our New Horizons can be attributed to a number of factors. First, of course, the need. But beyond that is Marge Mandel who has been its inspiration, its originator and facilitator. She has helped give New Horizons a spirit and sense of friendship that cannot be equaled. Her dedication to it is unmatched.

Then among its leadership have been men and women who have been in leadership capacities in other Temple activities and have willingly given their time and talent to New Horizons. New leadership of comparable ability has been developed.

Finally, a sense of a caring community was created. Programs were always interesting, dinners inviting, calling committees arranged, rides provided, and communication between members constantly improved. And it has brought new dedication to the Temple.

N.I.P.
The Neighborhood Involvement Program

Most of us recall the rioting in the cities during the summer of 1968 with its concomitant burning and looting. Among the causes for the outbursts, according to some of the leaders of the rioters, was the charge that the business people of their communities did not live there. They came from the suburbs, spent their day in the neighborhood, and then returned to the suburbs. They had no concerns for the people among whom they worked or from whom they derived their livelihoods.

Most of us remember how volatile the times were. No one could predict what would happen next or what would spark a conflict. Our Temple leadership worried whether our High Holy Day Services would be interrupted by some hostile group that year, and we made plans for that eventuality. I did not want anyone, anywhere in the city, to have the opportunity or the effrontery to make any statement against our Temple membership. Most of us did not live in the Temple neighborhood. Most of us did come to Temple from the suburbs and returned once a Service or Temple activity was concluded. But we did have a concern for the neighborhood. Our problem was how could we show it.

Burton Joseph was then our Temple president. Marvin Borman was our president elect. We asked Angelo Cohen, who was a long time resident of the neighborhood — he lives two blocks from the Temple — and a long time member of the congregation, to meet with us to explore the possibility of some kind of program. Angelo agreed to make inquiries and to think through the problem.

Unknown to us at the time, four churches in our neighborhood, Grace Presbyterian Church, St. Paul's Episcopal, Trinity Baptist, and Lake of the Isles Lutheran had formed an association called N.I.P. some two years before and had already embarked on a program. The basic idea of N.I.P. (Neighborhood Involvement Program) was for congregational volunteers to reach out into the neighboring community to provide whatever needs there might be. Ours was then a middle and low income community, with a goodly number of single parent families and many elderly in board and care homes. Jefferson Jr. High School was close by, and there were students who needed help. And so N.I.P. provided a clothes closet, a nursery school, summer camp programs, a tutoring service, evening instructional and activity programs, and a caring and social program for the elderly. All of the programs, with the exception of the camping, were held in the congregational buildings. All were financed by the churches. There was one paid worker, Judy Justad, the N.I.P. Director.

I discovered the program by accident. Ellen and Rudy Boschwitz had invited a group of "interesting people" from all parts of the county to their home for an evening, and the discussions ranged over all the issues affecting our country and community. At some point I mentioned what we at Temple hoped to do in our immediate neighborhood, and one of the guests described what his congregation was already accomplishing as a member of N.I.P. He was a congregant of Grace Presbyterian Church and served on N.I.P.'s Board.

Soon thereafter I was in touch with Rev. George Easley, the minister of Grace Church and President of N.I.P. It did not take our Board long to investigate what N.I.P. was doing, to approve the idea, to provide for our financial contribution to it, and to ask if we could join. On September 8, 1970 the Board of Trustees of N.I.P. accepted us as a member.

The idea of N.I.P. was novel not only to our area, but for the state. I had never heard of five congregations, four of different Protestant sects and one Jewish, who had banded together in an ecumenical program of outreach to their community. What made it exciting was that our memberships were to do the actual work, and our congregations were the sole financial support. The concept was pure religion in action for all of us.

Temple was the largest of the five congregations involved, and we entered the program wholeheartedly. Seymour Robinson was our first chairperson, and with help from his committee we soon had over one hundred volunteers offering their services. The N.I.P. Day Camp and Clothes Closet were placed in our building. I suggested two additional programs for N.I.P.: A Medical and Dental Clinic to be served by the physicians and dentists of our congregations, and an idea of upgrading the homes in our neighborhood which were old and which could easily deteriorate.

The Medical and Dental Clinic soon came to be. N.I.P. had purchased a building at 2636 Hennepin Avenue, and space was available. Dr. Gil Westreich, a Temple member, became the first Director of the Clinic, supplies from Mt. Sinai and Northwestern Hospitals were obtained, and the Clinic has been of great service to those in the area who have needed it. The home improvement idea remained just that, an idea. Fortunately, it did not have to be implemented. As home costs escalated, as the energy crisis increased, as our downtown was redeveloped, many of the homes in our immediate area were renovated, and the neighborhood became a desirable one for families once again.

In 1974, the five N.I.P. congregations were joined by a sixth, the Episcopal Cathedral of St. Marks, and that gave us another and new impetus. But even with that support, as N.I.P. programs expanded and as more professionals served on its staff, the budget exceeded by far what the congregations could contribute to it. Business foundations in the city and other agencies were appealed to for support. The United Way made us one of its beneficiaries, and though volunteerism has diminished, N.I.P. is still an agency of the congregations and is controlled by a Board of Trustees composed primarily of its members. Rabbi Barack served as its president from 1976 to 1977.

N.I.P. not only was our "good neighbor" policy but was a great personal source of pride for me, for the Temple and for all who contributed to it. I always felt a sense of elation at the expressions of awe when I would mention Temple's involvement in such a project to my colleagues. There are few congregations in the country, if any, that can emulate it.

ARZA

As we all know, the hostility of the Orthodox establishment in Israel and the political power it possesses has made the growth of Reform Judaism there slow and arduous.

I need not enumerate what Reform Judaism as a movement or what individuals who are members of Reform congregations have done for Israel. The Hebrew Union College-Jewish Institute of Religion has established a branch in Jerusalem, and every student preparing to be a Reform rabbi or educator must spend his first year there. The World Union of Progressive Judaism has placed its international headquarters in the same city. The Leo Baeck High School in Haifa is one of the most prestigious academic institutions in the country, and a Reform kibbutz is prospering in the Negev. There are today some thirteen Reform congregations in Israel, but the government still refuses to grant Reform Judaism, its institutions and rabbis, recognition.

Changes, though tortuous, are nevertheless inevitable. One reason is that ARZA, the Association of Reform Zionists of America, came into being at the Biennial Convention of the Union of American Hebrew Congregations in the fall of 1977. Its role is to mobilize the Reform Jews in the United States to exert maximum pressure on the Israel government so that Jewish religious pluralism will be officially recognized.

Temple Israel was among the first congregations in the country to establish a chapter of ARZA. In the first six months of its existence, with Fremajane Wolfson as our chairperson, Rabbi Roland Gittlesohn, president of ARZA and Rabbi Ira Youdovin, its Executive Director, came to Temple to speak from our pulpit. Judy Goldenberg, one of our Temple vice-presidents, has been appointed to the National Board of ARZA and attended its first convention.

Here is the Rabbi's Message introducing ARZA to the congregation:

July 5, 1977

I have just returned from the 88th Annual Convention of the Central Conference of American Rabbis and it was a historic meeting. The Conference voted to join with the Union of American Hebrew Congregations in support of ARZA, the Association of Reform Zionists of America.

ARZA is a new affiliate of the Union on a par with the National Federation of Sisterhoods, Brotherhoods, Youth, etc. It has come into being, at long last, because Reform Judaism has never had the voice and power it should have in the World Zionist Organization. None of the existing Zionist organizations, of which you may be members, express it — and the only religious influence in the WZO has been the Mizrachi, which is tied to the Orthodox National Religious Party in Israel.

What will ARZA do? It will enable Reform Judaism to speak out forcefully for Reform in Israel. It will give us a full voice and involve us in the inner circles of the Zionist organization. It will bring needed new perspectives and fresh leadership to it and underscore the essential pluralism in Jewish life.

Especially now is ARZA vital. The agreement that Menachem Begin has made with the Agudat Israel (the ultra-Orthodox party) in order to form a government, is reprehensible. He may turn back the clock regarding the "Who is a Jew?" question and, without doubt, there will be an intensification of discrimination against Reform and Conservative Judaism.

Every Reform Jew should join ARZA. Your vote will help give

Reform the strength it needs in Israel. Look elsewhere in this issue for the registration form, and God bless.

As ever,

The Dating Service

No one has to point out that the structure of the American Jewish community has greatly changed over the last quarter of a century. The move to the suburbs and to the warm states, the inclination of our young people to live away from home at an early age and often in parts of the country — or the world — far from their parents, the divorce rate, the tendency of young women to pursue careers, all these have contributed to disrupt the vaunted cohesiveness of the Jewish family. And even when they live in the same community it is not easy, once college days are over, to make new Jewish friends or meet other Jewish men and women of the same age. Over the years, both parents and young career people have come to me with the same question: How do we bring Jewish men and women together?

Every now and again we at Temple attempted a singles group for young people, but except for one some 25 years ago, they did not last more than a few months. I thought perhaps that computerized dating might be the answer, but that was far too complicated to try. Then one day it all fell into place.

I was meeting with a Bar Mitzvah parent, a woman who had been widowed and who was now happily remarried. "Rabbi," she said, "I don't know what I would have done if I had not met my present husband. I tried all the single things when I was alone, and they were a disaster. If someone had not made the effort to introduce us, I would be here with tears in my eyes instead of joy in my heart. I want to show my gratitude by helping other Jewish men and women to meet."

That began our Dating Service. I enlisted her help, and she with two friends began the task of interviewing and matching. This is the Rabbi's Message announcing the Service:

January 15, 1980

Twenty-five years ago, before it was an idea taken up by many other institutions, Temple Israel had a Singles Group that was community-wide in its appeal. It was vibrant and exciting, and many young people — especially those new to the city — came to its cultural and social events. I do not recall when our "group" came to an end, but it has been some years. Most recently the JCC has developed such a "group," and I am sure it fulfills the needs of many.

About fifteen years or so ago, we began a "Single Parents" group. It, too, was community-wide and was exceedingly well-received. It still exists at Temple as the "Jewish Singles" — because it expanded its focus — and it meets regularly and successfully for a variety of activities.

But something has been lacking. The "group," idea, good as it may be for some, is a dismal experience for others. And I have been wracking my brain for some way of bringing young Jewish men and women together. That there is a need is very evident to me.

Recently I have met with some women who are willing to help in establishing a Jewish Dating Service. We will center it at Temple. There will be no fee. It will be available to the entire community. All information will be kept scrupulously confidential.

We hope to personalize the computer approach with personal interviews and careful screening. All we ask is that those interested call the Temple and ask for Charlotte. She will answer your questions.

The idea may be a failure. But it may succeed. And we just have to try. After all, there is a Midrash that tells us "marriages are made in heaven," and our tradition insists that we are partners with God. We can't let Him down.

As ever,

* * * *

Our Dating Service, as you can see, was opened to the entire community and the results exceeded anything we dreamed of. In the first week there were almost 200 calls. I even had a call from New York from a woman who had somehow heard about it, and a number of rabbis from other parts of the country wrote, hoping to duplicate what we had done.

The women who were working the Dating Service had not

realized — nor had I — how time consuming the enterprise was. They called me a few weeks after we started (I was out of the city on a Sabbatical) informing me that the service was so extensive that it could no longer be accomplished on a volunteer basis. They felt that some compensation was necessary. I told them that it was too important an accomplishment to discontinue and that somehow — I had my Discretionary Fund in mind — I would find some financial help for them.

When I returned to the city, I discovered the extent of the Dating Service, the time they had given to it, and the compensation they felt it required. Though the Dating Service was fulfilling my hopes and though my Discretionary Fund could afford some funds, it just could not continue to provide the finances that were needed.

And so reluctantly, we turned the Dating Service over to the women who had worked it with our blessing. This is the announcement as it appeared in my "Rabbi's Message":

May 30, 1980

Early in January I wrote in this column that we, at Temple, with the help of three women from the community — one is a Temple member — were establishing a Jewish Dating Service. If you recall, I said that there would be no fee, that it would be available to all, and that it would be kept scrupulously confidential. "The idea may be a failure," I concluded, "but it may succeed. And we just have to try."

Well, our efforts exceeded every expectation. Almost 500 people have responded in the past five months and almost 800 dates have been arranged. Mothers have called to thank me for such a positive action, exuberant about the people their sons or daughters have met. Some who are personally involved have also called with similar comments. There may even be a few marriages in the offing.

The three women who have worked on the program have put in hundreds of hours, far beyond anything we anticipated. The time they spent was necessary. The kind of personal interest we intended demanded it. They now feel that the time they devote requires some compensation.

I estimate that over 90% of those who had registered are not from our congregation and that the service is truly a total community enterprise. What is clear is that my Rabbi's Discretionary Fund just cannot afford what must be done if it is to continue. There have been some tentative investigations toward bringing it under a Federation subsidized agency, but that has been unsucussful.

Be that as it may, we are turning the entire structure of the Jewish Dating Service over to the three women who have made it so worthwhile. We do it with our blessing. The Temple is no longer involved.

I am delighted that we started it, grateful that it made such a good beginning, and hopeful that it will continue to grow and serve.

As ever,

The Outreach Program

I need not tell you that there has been a startling increase in intermarriage over the past decade and that it is a phenomenom that is here to stay. Recent studies indicate that almost 40% of the Jewish men and women who marry, marry someone who was not born Jewish. About one-third of these choose to become Jewish, and most of them eventually join a congregation. Many of the other couples also intend to raise their children as Jews.

Each rabbi and each congregation has to respond in some way to this new trend in American Jewish life. There are some who will totally reject such a couple. There are others who will be indifferent or hostile to it. The Reform movement is on record as being welcoming and hospitable.

No rabbi can avoid confronting intermarriage. I serve as the chairperson of the Conversion Committee of the Central Conference of American Rabbis and as the co-chairperson of the Union of American Hebrew Congregation's Task Force on Reform Outreach. This is a Task Force established to study intermarriage and conversion in America and to recommend policy to the Union. Because of my involvement, and stimulated by our Task Force meetings, I organized an "Outreach Program" for Temple couples, one of whom was not Jewish. Following is the Rabbi's Message announcing it:

October 23, 1979

As some of you know, I am the co-chairperson of the National

Task Force on Outreach. It is a task force comprised of 23 individuals, nine of whom are Rabbis. The other persons are members of the Board of the Union of American Hebrew Congregations or have been carefully selected for their expertise or experience.

The Task Force was called together by Rabbi Alexander Schindler, president of the UAHC, for a number of purposes. However, our initial and present prime thrust is to develop a program for reaching out to intermarried couples, with the idea of bringing Jewish information and feeling to the partner who is not Jewish. What the result of such an outreach will be no one knows, but the hope is that such couples will become Jewishly knowledgeable; will rear their children as Jews; and, perhaps with the exposure we provide, the individual who is not Jewish will choose to become Jewish. There is to be no pressure or commitment while the process is in progress.

The entire concept and program is one which I consider to be among the most important undertaken by the Reform movement.

We are now trying to implement the idea and you have received some information in the mail. Please respond where you can. We need your help to make our efforts prosper.

As ever,

* * * *

That was the announcement. Now the results:

Some twenty couples responded, and we have begun to meet. Our meetings take place before a Jewish festival occurs so that it can be educational — an explanation of the holiday historically, ethically, traditionally and from a Reform perspective; and we have opened discussions on a variety of topics: Jewish children and non-Jewish grandparents; Jewish anti-Christian attitudes; anti-Semitism, synagogue attendance, in-laws, Christmas in the public schools, etc.

Though we may not be able to answer all questions or solve all the problems, there is no doubt that there is a need for such couples to come together to talk through their concerns, to learn from one another and the rabbi, and to experience the warmth and the welcoming of the congregation.

For the Record

Temple Israel on the National Scene

When I first came to Temple as the Assistant Rabbi in the summer of 1955, we were a congregation of some 750-800 families. In the last twenty-five years we have grown to over 1750 families and have become one of the leading congregations in the Reform Movement.

It is not only the size of our congregation that has brought us to this point, but the leadership we have provided.

In 1959 Rabbi Minda was elected Vice-President of the Central Conference of American Rabbis. He served two years in that position and two years as President of the Conference. Concomitant with his presidency of the CCAR he was a vice-president of the World Union for Progressive Judaism.

In 1968 I became the President of the newly formed Midwest Association of Reform Rabbis. Rabbi Barack was president from 1976 to 1977.

In 1972 I was elected President of the Rabbinic Alumni Association of the Hebrew College-Jewish Institute of Religion. I served on the Board of Governors of the College-Institute for six years and thereafter was appointed to the Rabbinic Board of Overseers in which capacity I still serve. From 1975 to 1977 I was Secretary of the Central Conference of American Rabbis and served on its Executive Board. Rabbi Barack served on that Board in 1976-77.

Bill Cardozo, one of our past presidents, served on the Board of the Union of American Hebrew Congregations from 1958-62, and Marvin Borman, also a past president, was a member of that Board from 1975-79.

Burton Joseph, another past president, has served on the Board of Governors of the Hebrew Union College-Jewish Institute of Religion since 1971. In 1975 he was elected a vice-president.

Gerry Friedell and Barry Graceman, both former Men's Club presidents, have served on the Board of the National Federation of Temple Brotherhoods. And Margie Graceman, Susie Selcer and Marge Mandel, all past Sisterhood presidents, as well as Frances Minda, have been on the Board of the National Federation of Temple Sisterhoods. Marge is a member of the Board of Overseers of the Cincinnati School of HUC-JIR as well.

Our Sisterhood has also played a most significant role in the

Midwest Federation of Temple Sisterhoods. Many of our Sisterhood members have served on the Midwest's Board of Trustees over the years and Corinne Birnberg, Gert Glass, Jo Jaffee, Roz Jaffee, Marge Mandel, Ardene Meshbesher, Lois Rose, Susie Selcer, and Betty Howard Tunick have been selected to the Executive Board. One of the great thrills of my rabbinate was to travel to the Convention of the Midwest Federation in April 1980 to install Lois Rose as its president. It was the first time in the 102-year-history of our congregation that a Temple member had reached that status in a national or regional group.

Our young people, too, have had a primary place in the Reform Movement. In 1975 Gary Birnberg was elected a vice-president of the Northern Federation of Temple Youth (NOFTY) and simultaneously served as a Board member of the National Federation of Temple Youth (NFTY). He became president of NOFTY in 1976-77.

In 1977-78 Sam Lieberman was NOFTY vice-president, in 1978-79 NOFTY secretary, and in 1979-80 he served as a vice-president of NFTY.

Steve Leder served as president of NOFTY from 1977-78; Beth Golden was treasurer and Leslie Segal editor of the NOFTY newsletter, "Kesh." Beth became president of NOFTY in 1978-79 and Liz Rose served under her as a vice-president. Jan Dann and Robin Apple were the "Kesh" editors.

Greg Leder became NOFTY president in 1979-80. Serving with him were Sheri Salloway and Jan Dann, vice-presidents and Sue Cohen, Secretary. Bran Klein was elected NOFTY Treasurer for 1980-81.

The Temple Building

Our Temple building is a magnificent structure that opened its doors in September of 1928. Jack Liebenberg was its architect, and he served on our Board of Trustees for many years, eventually becoming President of the congregation in 1965. What is more, he also served as a kind of "architect in residence," always searching for ways in which to enhance the beauty of the building and increase its efficiency.

Over the years there have been a number of changes in our

original building. Two were structural. In 1963 a new foyer was attached to our north entrance. This contained not only an additional office and elevator, but a desperately needed new meeting room, the Levitt Room. In 1966 the Sisterhood Reading Room was added to our Kaufman Library.

Internally, the corridors of the lower two floors were paneled, the Deinard Chapel and the Cardozo room constructed, additional office space and an audio-visual room created. There were also some changes in the Sanctuary. In 1958, the bema was expanded to make room for two lecturns, one for the rabbis, the other for the cantor. They replaced the original center lecturn. In addition, a centre aisle and centre steps for the bema were also installed. The Ark was refurbished, and for the first time carpet was laid along the Sanctuary aisles covering the original terrazzo floor.

The original Temple building was designed to house our Religious School, and it did so most adequately for almost a quarter of a century. By 1953 our school population had outgrown our facilities and the need for a Religious School building was obvious. In the summer of 1955 ground was broken for a new building which was to be united with the Temple proper, and in September, 1956, its doors were opened for the school year.

As you know, the Temple and Religious School building stand on a two block site between 22nd and 24th Streets and between Emerson and Fremont Avenues. As our Board of Trustees began to consider the future of the Temple, it was evident that should we need to expand, some of the homes in the area, most of which were old and in poor condition, would have to be purchased. Provisions were made, and gradually and fortunately many of the homes were acquired. Eventually the space was used to provide us with a much needed expanded parking lot and the opportunity, if it would become necessary, to add to our buildings.

By 1968 it was painfully clear that some extensive refurbishing had to be done in our original structure. The pews in the Sanctuary were no longer suitable, and the interior had not been painted in forty years. Our sound system was in need of improvement. Minda Hall needed completed renovation, and the gymnasium which had served the congregation and the community so well for so many years was completely inadequate and no longer in use. And there was desperate need for more parking space.

Then began the analysis of our situation and its debate within our Board. If you recall, it was a time when some inner cities were in flames, and Minneapolis itself was tense. There were marches and protests and destruction on our North Side. In some places in the country, church services had been interrupted by hostile groups; and we could not be certain whether the Temple neighborhood would deteriorate to a point beyond recall and follow the course of so many other inner city communities.

The discussion was intense and spirited.

There were some who pleaded that it was time to move to the suburbs, and they made cogent arguments. There were those who could not conceive of Temple Israel in a different building in a different place. Others were uncertain, though sure that something had to be done. After much deliberation, our Board decided to stay where we were, and for three primary reasons: (1) It was felt that a downtown Jewish presence and voice in Minneapolis was essential; (2) Temple was not merely a city or county congregation. Its membership was statewide and beyond. We had congregants in St. Cloud, in Crookston, in Faribault, Burnsville, Huntington, Hibbing, and Eau Claire. More and more of our members were moving far beyond the city limits. Fortunately the site which was selected for our building in 1928 was not only centrally located, but was at the confluence of much of our highway system; (3) To build the kind of structure our congregation would need would require a staggering sum of money.

Once that decision was made, others had to follow. What would we do with our Sanctuary and halls? How could we renovate and modernize and maintain our impressive beauty? And there were two other considerations of equal importance to me: how could we at Temple somehow spur a home improvement program in our immediate area; and beyond that, what kind of neighbor did we as an institution aspire to be? Most of our membership did not live in the Temple neighborhood. Nonetheless, we, as a Temple community, had an obligation to it.

We began to address ourselves to both problems simultaneously.*

---

*See section on N.I.P., page 172.

Our immediate need was in our social halls and our parking. Jack Liebenberg, with a committee, was on hand to design and direct the renovation of Minda Hall. The floor of the gymnasium was raised, and a most functional hall called Joseph Auditorium, after I.S. Joseph, a past president, was presented to Temple by the Joseph family. It joined Minda Hall, and the two together gave us ample space for most Temple social and cultural activities.

A committee headed by Lou Gainsley and Marvin Wolfenson saw to it that some of our homes on Fremont Avenue and 22nd Street were razed, and a parking lot almost sufficient for our High Holy Day needs was constructed.

Now it was the moment to renovate the Sanctuary, and that took much more time, much more thought and much more care.

A small committee, chaired by Bob Weil, was given the task of developing the plans and supervising the work. It solicited ideas from a number of sources, sifted through many suggestions and opinions, and its final decisions are what you see as you enter our building today.

You can scarcely imagine my feelings when in July of 1977 I came into the Sanctuary to find all the pews removed, the aisle carpeting gone and scaffolding reaching to the ceiling. I could not fathom how it all would look, how the new colors would blend, how the congregation would respond. Bit by bit the painters painstakingly worked on our beautiful ceiling. Gradually the gold ornaments that were part of the design and had been obscured by the dust over the years came to light once again with a brilliance that was dazzling. In all this time I had not known what the ceiling had looked like in its original splendor. The bema was expanded once again with magnificent new lecterns and colorful benches for seating. The Ark was reconstructed. Finally, the Sanctuary floor was completely carpeted, the new pews fixed in place, new doors affixed, fire safety devices, new lighting and sound systems installed, and the old organ which had served us so well and for so long but which was beginning to wheeze and to cough, was replaced. By the fall of 1978, our hundredth anniversary as a congregation and the fiftieth anniversary of the construction of our Temple, the building was ready.

To accomplish all that we had set out to do and had finally completed required substantial funds. The Board voted a Development Fund, with the hope of financing not only the renovating and reconstruction of our Temple building but also of erecting an adult facility at the Temple camp, and of giving impetus to our Endowment Fund which had been dormant for many years. All agreed that a substantial Fund would be a hedge against inflation and would permit us to continue our extensive programs without curtailment, and perhaps even give us the means to add new ones.

The Yom Kippur War erupted just as we were beginning our drive, and because we would not solicit the congregation while Israel's needs were greater than ever, we stopped our efforts. The impetus was never regained, and though we were able to complete the work at Temple, our other projects were placed in abeyance.

Though our needs continue to grow, we somehow seem to "make do," buoyed by the knowledge that our Sanctuary is beautiful and inviting, our Social Halls large and impressive, and our School Building and Camp adequate. Further expansion and improvement is part of our future.

The Centennial Year

When a definitive history of Temple Israel is written, our 100th Anniversary celebration may be just one of a number of important events, but for those of us who planned and participated in it or merely enjoyed it, it was one of the highlights of our association with Temple.

Stanley Schweitzer was our Temple president in 1978-79, and he appointed Marge and Don Graceman as the general chairpersons for the Centennial year. Don and Marge gathered a representative committee together, and it set to work.

Three major events were planned: one to mark our 100th Annual Meeting; the second, a weekend consisting of a Confirmation Reunion and a Civic Dinner; and the third to conclude the year with our 101st Annual Meeting. There were to be other happenings as well, and when the entire year's program was finally developed, something special had been designated for almost every month of the year.

Elliot Kaplan, our president-elect and Winky Herman, our Sisterhood president took over the planning of our 100th Annual

Meeting which fell on May 26. The meeting took the form of a Friday evening Service, and I compiled a special Sabbath worship for it. Our speaker was the Honorable Simcha Dinitz, the Israeli Ambassador to the United States. Ambassador Dinitz did not generally speak for congregations. You can imagine how many invitations he would have received, how many he would have had to refuse, and how much disappointment he would thereby generate. He came to us as a special favor to Burton Joseph, a past president of the Temple and who was, in 1978, national president of the Anti-Defamation League.

It was a wonderful evening. The Temple was filled to capacity, and a beautiful Oneg Shabbat followed.

In September, as close as we could manage to the date of the founding of Temple a hundred years before, there was an outstanding weekend. It began with the Confirmation Reunion on Friday, September 8, 1978. Lois Rose chaired the committee for the occasion, and she and her workers contacted and invited Temple confirmands from every part of the country. Many came. The Temple was more beautiful than ever that evening, confirmands from every generation, including our oldest living confirmand, Marion Bearman of the class of 1914, participated in the Service and the Oneg Shabbat was a thrilling homecoming for everyone there.

The last evening, Saturday, September 9, was the occasion of our Civic Dinner. It was held at the Radisson South Hotel, and some 1000 people were present. Distinguished guests from the community had been invited, and they sat at a two tier head table. It was a joyous evening, and everyone was resplendent.

Marvin Borman was the chairperson for the dinner, and because of him and other members of the congregation, Vice President Walter Mondale had agreed to be our speaker. He had not appeared at any such event anywhere since his election, and much excitement surrounded his coming.

On the Friday afternoon of our Confirmation Reunion, some thirty-six hours before the Civic Dinner, Burt Joseph and I were invited to the Boone-Erickson Radio talk show to discuss Temple and the 100th Anniversary. I came into the WCCO studio a bit early, introduced myself to the receptionist and was prepared to wait for Burt, but I did not get the chance. "Rabbi Shapiro," the receptionist gasped, "the Vice President of the United States has been trying to reach you," and she handed me a message and directed me to a desk from where I could call Washington.

Now I had known Vice President Mondale for some time. My association began when I was a member of the State Commission Against Discrimination, and he was the Attorney General. However, I had not spoken to him for some months and never before had I put in a call to a Vice President of the country. It was with some emotion and trepidation that I dialed the number and heard his voice.

You all know the story. "Camp David was in progress and the President wanted him there for the weekend to help in the ongoing negotiations. He was terribly sorry. Could he send a tape recording of some remarks."

Fortunately, the Vice President's absence did not dampen the beauty and the exhilaration of the evening. There was a tape from the Vice President, and his wife, Joan, made a surprise appearance and spoke briefly. A documentary history of Temple was shown, the speakers were brisk and spontaneous, and a dance concluded the evening. The "success" of the two days — the Confirmation Reunion and the Civic Dinner — exceeded our every hope.

The Annual Meeting and the weekend celebrations were only a beginning. In October the New Horizons Group sponsored "An Evening of Nostalgia" on the last day of Sukkot. In November our annual Thanksgiving Service with seven downtown congregations took place at Temple to the delight of all, and in December the Sisterhood and Men's Club, with the help of the Couples Club, provided us with the "Big Show '78," a musical review in which 200 Temple performers and workers gave us three sparkling performances. In December also, we honored our Daily Worship Readers and "Shamuses" with a dinner and Sabbath Service.

Two Friday evening speakers highlighted the Centennial year for us. The ever popular Al Vorspan, Vice-President of the Union of American Hebrew Congregations, spoke in October. And in January Rabbi Herbert S. Rutman of Har Zion Congregation in Baltimore spoke. As most of you remember, Rabbi Rutman was our Associate Rabbi from 1965-1973. He brought with him a resolution from the city of Baltimore saluting Temple on its 100th Anniversary. That document plus one from the Union of American Hebrew Congregations, one from the State of Minnesota and another from Hennepin County now hangs in our Kaplan gallery.

The Centennial year concluded with another notable weekend. On April 27, 1979, a Yom Kippur-size congregation came to hear Rabbi W. Gunther Plaut at a Friday evening Service. Rabbi Plaut, the author of "The Jews of Minnesota" and a former rabbi at our sister congregation in St. Paul gave us a spirited talk on the early days of Temple. The following Sunday evening our 101st Anniversary was observed with a dinner meeting. All those who had helped make the year so meaningful were thanked, and Elliot Kaplan succeeded Stanley Schweitzer as president of the congregation as we moved into the second century of our existence.

Here are some Rabbi's Messages I wrote during the Centennial Year:

June 13, 1978

May 26 seemed like such a long way off when Ambassador Simcha Dinitz accepted our invitation to speak at our 100th Annual Meeting. And now it is behind us.

I need not tell the more than 1,000 of you who were present how impressive and beautiful the evening was. So many of you have called to tell me that the Service I wrote was touching and inspiring; the words of Stanley Schweitzer, Elliot Kaplan, Don Graceman and Burt Joseph so meaningful; and the message of the ambassador forthright and sobering. And the Oneg Shabbat could not have been more beautiful. That was the work of Winky Herman.

But an evening such as May 26 does not happen by itself. So there are many who deserve our gratitude. There is Stanley Schweitzer, our Temple President, and Elliot Kaplan, president-designate (Elliot and Winky were the co-chairpersons of the evening). There are the 65 men and women who served as hosts and hostesses. Marvin Kahner had 25 ushers with him. Walter Baron watched over everything. And my secretary, Melinda, put many of the minutiae of the day together. Every detail was just right.

But there are three people without whom all the other planning would have been in vain. It was Burt Joseph who extended the invitation to the ambassador. And it was Marge and Don Graceman, who gathered together all the strands and gave us the memorable occasion.

For all of us, I say thank you to all of them.

As ever,

* * * *

July 12, 1978

In just a few weeks you will begin to receive invitations to three forthcoming Centennial events. The Couples Club is planning a Temple picnic for August 27, a Confirmation Reunion Service has been set for September 8 and our Centennial Civic-Night Dinner will take place on September 9.

In planning our major Centennial celebrations, our committee followed two courses. One, we determined to have a number of internal events that would reach out to the entire congregation at no cost to any of our members. One such was our 100th Anniversary Service at which Ambassador Dinitz spoke. The Temple Picnic and Confirmation Reunion will be others.

Then we planned our Centennial Dinner. This is to be not only for our Temple membership, but for the community, both Jewish and general. The governor, the mayor, our United States Senators, Congressmen Frazer and Frenzel, Archbishop Roach, Bishop Anderson, U of M President Dr.C. Peter Magrath, Matthew Ross (Chairman of the Board of the Union of American Hebrew Congregations), and others have accepted our invitation. And I am delighted to tell you that Vice President Mondale will be our speaker for the evening. It indicates his esteem for our congregation and is a singular honor for us.

Our committee also thought that the occasion should be more festive than just dinner and program, so we decided that dancing would be part of the evening's fare.

September 9 undoubtedly will be another high point in our year's activity and in Temple history. Please place the date on your calendar now.

As ever,

* * * *

May 15, 1979

Our Centennial year concluded during the weekend of April 27-29 with a spirit and sense of purpose that was uplifting and inspiring. No one could have asked for more.

On Friday evening, a Yom Kippur-size congregation heard Rabbi W. Gunther Plaut, author of "The Jews of Minnesota," capsulate the story of Temple Israel as it has never been done before. He did it with humor, with scholarly analysis, and with an inspirational message. The Oneg Shabbat that followed was festive.

On Sunday evening, the 101st Annual Meeting capped the year with seriousness, song and a heart-warming feeling of friendship and delight. Stanley Schweitzer's presidential address focused on the achievements of the last two years and on our request to the Federation for Temple's educational needs. It was a forthright and meaningful statement. Elliot Kaplan, our new Temple president, laid out for us the challenges the year ahead must inevitably bring and the responsibility the Temple and the entire community has in facing them.

Marge and Don Graceman, our Centennial co-chairpersons, summed up the year with just the right touch, and Margie presented Elliot with a volume of all the names of the members of Temple of the Centennial year.

Then Suzie Selcer, the chairperson for the evening, introduced Margie Belkin, Liz Joseph and Raleigh Kuller, with Fran Finkelstein at the piano, who regaled us with a Centennial skit that had us howling with laughter and singing for joy.

It was a memorable evening, and thanks go to all who planned and participated in it, all who made the year such a super success.

As ever,

Hubert H. Humphrey

Honors are the perquisites of the clergy. In any other form of work or service, a man or a woman may achieve the highest success, but rarely do they receive public acknowledgement, acclamation or honor from peers or patients, from clients or consumers. But a rabbi — that is different! No rightful honor passes him or her by, should he/she have had the good fortune of being in a community or a congregation for a goodly number of years.

As you know, I have had that good fortune, and I have had my share of public honor. But perhaps the greatest reward given me was when I was asked to participate in the funeral service of our late and beloved Hubert Humphrey.

We were all aware of the cancer that was ravaging Senator Humphrey. We all knew his days were limited. And he, too, knew that he was soon to die. And so with his usual foresight he, his family and Dr. Calvin Didier, the Minister of the House of Hope Presbyterian Church in St. Paul, planned his funeral. He requested that Archbishop John Roach represent the Catholic community and that I represent the Jewish community. I was unaware that this was his wish.

On the morning after the Senator's death, I had a telephone call from his office. Would I participate in the Service.

Most of you recall the Service which was televised nationally. Though there had also been a Service in Washington the day before, President Carter, Vice President Mondale, the leadership of the Senate and dignitaries from all over the country came once again to pay tribute and respect to this great American. As Bernice and I came to the church at least an hour before the Service was to begin, we could see the thousands that were already lining the streets despite the freezing weather. Inside the church every possible space was filled, every room crowded with family and invited friends.

Though you may recall the Service, I doubt whether you remember my part in it. It was almost a disaster.

I use three pair of glasses: one for driving; one for reading; and a third that combines something of the first two. I wear it on the pulpit. It permits me to read, and it lets me see most of the congregation. With my "reading" glasses I could not see beyond the prayer book. With my "driving" glasses I could not see the prayerbook.

At the time I was asked to participate in the Service, my all purpose glasses were being repaired, and there was no way to retrieve them. So I was faced with a dilemma: I needed my "seeing" glasses to walk to the lecturn without stumbling or shuffling. I needed my reading glasses to see what had to be read. And I did not want to be up there juggling two pair of glasses. So I did what turned out to be best. I groped to the pulpit without glasses, carrying the reading glasses in my hand. Once on safe ground, I adjusted them and said the following:

Hubert Humphrey was my friend, just as he was yours. Many a time we were together. Many a time I watched him enter an auditorium to resounding applause and leave it to a standing ovation. Many a time I greeted him and said goodby. Now for the last time, and for all of us, I say farewell as I read from Psalm VIII:

"O Lord, our Lord,
How glorious is Thy name in all the earth.
When I behold Thy heavens, the
 work of Thy fingers,
The moon and the stars which Thou
 hast established.
What is man that Thou art mindful of him?
Or the son of man that Thou thinkest of him?
Yet Thou hast made him but little lower
 than the angels,
And hast crowned him with glory and honor.
Thou hast made him to have dominion over the
 works of Thy hands,
Thou hast put all things under his feet:
Sheep and oxen, all of them,
Yea, and the beasts of the field;
The fowl of the air, and the fish of the sea,
Whatsoever passeth through the paths of the seas.
O Lord, our Lord,
How glorious is Thy name in all the world."

For many days after the Service I had telephone calls and mail from all parts of the country. Some said they had not recognized me immediately because I was not wearing glasses. Everyone expressed pride that "their rabbi" had been part of this historic, though sad, occasion. The most unexpected call was from Dr. Henry Bloom, long retired and living in Florida. Dr. Bloom had been a neighbor of ours when we lived in Winthrop, Massachusetts. I had not seen or heard from him in some thirty years.

A Final Personal Note

In June, 1960, I earned a Doctor's Degree in Education from the University of Cincinnati, and I owe it all to the United States government and Bernice Shapiro.

It happened this way. When I entered the Hebrew Union College in 1955 I was a veteran with the maximum allowance under the G.I. Bill of Rights. So not only were tuition payments made for me, but books were provided; and because I was married with two small children, I received a stipend of $120.00 each month.

As the summer of 1956 approached, it was necessary for me to find a job for the summer months: "No schooling, no government stipend." Fortunately it was not difficult. The Jewish Community Center of Cincinnati offered me the position of Youth Director for the summer. My salary, the going rate in those days, was to be $300 for the season. It sounded perfect, but for some reason which I cannot now remember, I decided to check with the University of Cincinnati, and this is what I discovered. If I took a full course — 12 credits each summer term — the G.I. Bill would provide my monthly allowance, and there would still be provision for my years at the Hebrew Union College. Now, 24 credits for the summer is much, but the fact was that I would be paid more for going to school than for working for the Community Centre. No one ever had a better uncle than Uncle Sam!

I finished the summer session with 4 "A's" and 2 "B's" and enrolled in the University the following summer under the same conditions. My classes were in the Graduate School of Education because I already had a Masters Degree in that field and Jewish Education was one of my major interests. But I had no thoughts of earning a degree.

As you may know, each student at the Graduate School is assigned an advisor. Mine called me in at the end of that second summer. "You now have 48 credits," he informed, me, "and all we require is 75 credits beyond a Masters Degree for a doctorate. If you continue for another summer and take one fall-winter semester you will have it made. All that will be necessary will be the passing of examinations and a dissertation."

It seemed easy enough. And it was very exciting. I speculated that I could earn a doctors degree from the University and be ordained at the Hebrew Union College the same month of the same year. No one had ever done that before.

I finished my course work. I passed my exams. The proposal for my dissertation was accepted. I was sure that my last year at the College and my biweekly pulpits (the rabbinic students serve congregations in the small communities within a 500 or so mile radius of Cincinnati every other week) would not interfere with my research and writing. But it was not to be.

Rockdale Ave. Temple of Cincinnati, one of the great congregations in the country, suddenly needed a Director for its Religious School — a School with about 1000 students. I was offered the position, and from a financial point of view it was one I could not refuse. But it was impossible to do it well while finishing H.U.C. and writing a dissertation. One had to go, and it was the latter. But I pledged to myself that I would complete the doctorate during my first year as a rabbi. And that, too, was not to be.

I had no idea what it meant to be a rabbi, how much time would be required, how many meetings there were to attend, how many people there were to see. So the first year passed and Bernice noted that the dissertation languished. The second year passed and she "noodged" a bit. The third year also passed, but with the fourth she insisted. And as almost always happens, she had her way. Every spare moment that summer, fall and winter was spent in reading and writing. By February my first draft was submitted to my Committee at the University, and in May I was informed that I would be awarded the degree at the June commencement, 1960. Commencement came, but Bernice and I just could not make the trip to Cincinnati. The diploma arrived in the mail some weeks later.

I was now a "doctor." But I wrote then and I repeat now that I would not use the title or even the letters the degree indicates next to my name. For me the title "rabbi" is the most meaningful that I could attain.

Now I have a second doctorate — the honorary Doctor of Divinity degree conferred upon me by my seminary, the Hebrew Union College-Jewish Institute of Religion. This comes not because of the U.S. government but because of Bernice and you, the Temple congregation. She and you have made the rabbinate a beautiful fulfilling career for me.

*   *   *   *

Friday and Saturday, June 13 and 14, were two days that Bernice and I shall never forget. It was our 25th Anniversary at Temple, and as you know, our Board of Trustees decided to make it a congregational celebration.

For Bernice and me it was more exciting than we had anticipated. Our entire family came — Susan from London, Bernice's mother from Atlanta, my two brothers, Dr. Joe and Rabbi Robert and their wives, Harriet and Charlotte, and my sister Sylvia from Boston. Steven, our son, lives in town. So all that were lacking — besides nieces and nephews — were Sylvia's husband, Mike, who could not get away, Susan's husband, Dan, in London, and our nine-month-old grandson, Zachary, whom we left at home with a babysitter.

Here is the Rabbi's Message which could only begin to express our thanks for the Friday evening Service, the Saturday evening dinner, and the dedication of our Religious School as the Rabbi Max A. Shapiro Education Building:

July 1, 1980

It was a perfect two days for Bernice and me. From the opening hymn of the Service on Friday eve to the closing benediction on Saturday night, it was more than we could have anticipated or expected.

I must tell you that on Friday afternoon I began to get nervous. Suppose, I thought, just suppose that with all the preparations, and the four prominent speakers, suppose that only a handful of people came. After all, it is June, the sun is hot, the lakes and golf courses beckoning. But the Temple, as you know, was full — and when, after I completed my remarks, you all rose and applauded, it was overwhelming. I did not know which way to turn or what to say. After all, whoever heard of applause at a Temple Service!

And then, Saturday night. Do you know that the dinner was originally planned for Minda Hall? That the Temple would be full on Friday eve was a possibility, but who could have foreseen Saturday. Almost 700 of you crowded into the Hotel de France. There were over 100 letters expressing regrets, and I do not know how many were turned away. All of us are sorry that there was not enough space for everyone, and that some of you had to be seated on the extreme fringes of the room.

But the Hotel did extend itself to serve us all so well, and then the program! Bill Cardozo was great; my brother, Bob, sensational; Elliot Kaplan and Sid Cohen had the right touches; and I can't find a word in the dictionary or Thesaurus to describe Liz Joseph, Marge Belkin and Raleigh Kuller (with Fran Finkelstein at the piano). I'll just make one up. "Superexcelperfessence."

To all the others who helped make the two days possible — a great big thanks.

As ever,

Appendix

Rabbinic Leadership

Rabbis of Temple Israel

Henry Friedman Schreiber	1878-1880
Henry Illiowizi	1880-1888
Samuel Marks	1888-1893
Aaron Friedman	1893-1901
Samuel N. Deinard	1901-1921
Albert G. Minda	1922-1963
Emeritus	1963-1977
Max A. Shapiro	1963-

Assistant and Associate Rabbis

Richard Singer	1945-1947
Leonard Devine	1948-1950
Max A. Shapiro	1955-1957
Associate	1957-1963
Jay B. Goldburg	1963-1965
Herbert S. Rutman	1965-1967
Associate	1967-1973
Stephan F. Barack	1973-
Associate	
Daniel G. Zemel	1979-

Presidents of Temple Israel

Leopold Ehrlich
Edward Bernstein
Ralph Rees
Jacob Skoll
Joseph Kantrowitz
Abraham Stromberg
Isaac Weil
Henry Weiskopf
Max W. Frank
Emile Adelsheim
Jonas Weil
I.H. Robitshek
Ralph M. Hamburger
I.S. Joseph

P.B. Juster
Charles R. Goldstein
Joseph D. Lipkin
Charles R. Goldstein *(one year)*
William N. Cardozo
Jack J. Liebenberg
Charles R. Glass
Burton M. Joseph
Marvin Borman
Edwin F. Harris
Sidney R. Cohen
Stanley Schweitzer
Elliot S. Kaplan

Sisterhood Presidents

Bertha Weiskopf	1903-1906	Lillian Grodnik	1952-1954
Ida Heller	1906-1919	Marjorie Graceman	1954-1958
Lillie Mikolas	1919-1922	Gertrude R. Glass	1958-1960
Stella Schloss	1922-1926	Marjorie L. Marks	1960-1962
Lillie Mikolas	1926-1929	Suzanne Selcer	1962-1966
Anna Goldberg	1929-1932	Doris Rose	1966-1970
Leona Wilmer	1932-1934	Marjorie Mandel	1970-1972
Ruth Litin	1934-1939	Lois Rose	1972-1974
Edythe Beugen	1939-1942	Corrinne Birnberg	1974-1976
Dorothy Banks	1942-1946	Ruth Schneider	1976-1978
Ruth Pritikin	1946-1947	Winky Herman	1978-1980
Gertrude Mayeron	1947-1950	Myrna Abrams	1980-
Betty Howard	1950-1952		

Presidents of the Men's Club

Irving Robitshek
P.B. Juster
Hans Brecher
Harold R. Kaufmann, Sr.
Lewis L. Perlman
William F. Friedman
Sam Levy
Max Levy
Arthur A. Segal
S. Harry Gainsley
Donald D. Graceman
Gerald M. Robbins
Bernard Edelman
Elliott B. Hoffman
Louis S. Sinykin
Stanley V. Shanedling
Joseph H. Bonoff

Seymour Silverberg
Joseph Kates
Irving Apple
Marvin Borman
Leo Dorfman
Norman Diamond
Gerald H. Friedell
Lawrence G. Greenberg
Chester V. Grossman
Robert I. Weil
Stanley H. Schweitzer
Stuart Belkin
Irving Hork
Martin Finch
Sheldon Kieffer
Barry Graceman
David Abramson

Presidents of the Couples' Club

Harold and Harriet Rutstein
Dr. Jacob and Bernice Berg
Dr. Harvey and Lee Moral
Dr. Sidney and Phyllis Chucker
Phillip and Shirley Dolinger
Dale and Toby Feiges
Bing and Barb Kaufman
Howard and Diane Kaplan
Dr. John and Ann Lonstein

New Horizons Presidents

Ray I. Bart
Jesse Rhodes

Temple Youth Group and Senior Youth Program Presidents

Steve Cook	1952-53	Dan Mandel	1972-73
Richard Howard	1959-60	Debbie Klein	1973-74
Fred Rosenblatt	1960-62	Jessica Gibson	1974-75
John Halpern	1962-63	Harry Brown	1975-76
Terry Tilsen	1964-65	John Rubenstein	1976-77
Debbie Diamond	1966-67	Julie Spiegel	1977-78
Sandra Braman	1968-69	Larry Westreich	1978-79
Naomi Kahn	1969-70	Amy Spiegel	1979-80
Peter Gray	1971-72	Debbie Rappaport	1980-81

Temple Administrators

Joseph Kahn
Zola Dockman
Walter Baron

Directors of Religious Education

Harry Glasser	Sidney Weisberg
Charles Marks	Rabbi Joseph Levine
Marshall Kaner	Joanne Glosser
Mansour Alyshmereni	

Directors of Nursery School

Roz Bearman	Dorothy Sipkins
Ceil Rozman	Joanne Blindman

Librarian

Georgia Kalman

Youth Directors

Harry Glasser
Robert Fisher
Paul Kent

Andy Halper
Larry Glosser
Rabbi Daniel Zemel

Directors of Camp Teko

Richard Singer
Harry Glasser
Sheila Glass
Jan Podoloff
Merrill Fishbein
Jack Mayeron

Gay Rosenthall
Steven Goldstein
Andy Halper
Steven Field
Larry Glosser
Jeffrey Goldstein

Photos

The Temple Israel Sanctuary as it was in 1955 when I arrived . . .

. . . and as it appears today, 25 years later.

My installation as Senior Rabbi in October, 1963. Standing with me are Bernice, our son Steven, and to my right Rabbi Roland Gittelsohn and my brother Rabbi Robert Shapiro, both of whom participated in the Service. Susan, our daughter, was also present.

The Deinard Memorial Chapel as it appeared when I first came to Temple.

With Senator Hubert H. Humphrey.

Senator Walter Mondale, my brother Rabbi Robert, and Mayor Arthur Naftalin came for my tenth anniversary at Temple in 1965.

With University of Minnesota President Malcolm Moos, Burton Joseph, and two members of the Board of Regents prior to a service honoring the University.

With Dr. Nelson Glueck, President of the Hebrew Union College, who ordained me and later became a good friend.

With Governor Harold LeVander on our return with the group representing the State of Minnesota at the funeral of Martin Luther King, Jr.

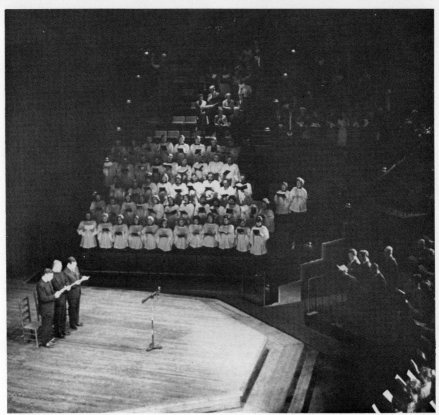

Sir Tyrone Guthrie wanted a religious
service to dedicate the Guthrie Theatre.
It was a highlight for me.

A SERVICE OF DEDICATION

THE TYRONE GUTHRIE THEATRE

Sunday, May 5, 1963 • 2:00 p.m.

OFFICIATING:

Rt. Rev. Msgr. James P. Shannon
President, College of St. Thomas

Rabbi Max A. Shapiro
Temple Israel

Rev. William R. Snyder
Senior Pastor, St. John's Lutheran Church

PARTICIPATING:

The Choir of St. John's Lutheran Church
Robert Hotvet, Directing

The Minnesota Theatre Company

A community Thanksgiving Service at the Temple. Represented were The Cathedral of St. Mark, The Basilica of St. Mary, Westminster Presbyterian, Hennepin Methodist, Plymouth Congregational, First Christian, and Wesley Methodist Churches.

An ecumenical service at Temple protesting Russian restrictions upon Jews. Joining me were Rabbi Herbert Rutman, Archbishop John Byrnes, Dr. John Cummins, and Dr. Melvin Hammerburg, President of the Minnesota Council of Churches.

Dr. Alfred Gottschalk, President of the Hebrew Union College/Jewish Institute of Religion, presents me with an honorary Doctor of Divinity degree in March, 1980.

With Richard Bluestein, President of the National Jewish Hospital in Denver, on receiving the Humanitarian Award from the hospital, December 1978.

Rabbi Arthur Lelyveld (center), President of the Central Conference of American Rabbis, came to speak at the Jewish National Fund dinner in my honor (1976). With us is my brother, Rabbi Robert.

I always performed at one of our "Big Shows." Here I am at rehearsal.

At my 60th birthday party given by the Sisterhood. With me are Bernice, our son Steven, and Mary Nadler.

t a Temple Passover Seder, I am distributing gifts to these youngsters after they found the afikomen.

With Ed Harris, Temple past president, and both national and local members of the Jewish National Fund in October 1977, in recognition of the Rabbi Max A. Shapiro Forest planted in Israel. Ed was chairperson of the Minnesota JNF Board.

Bernice and I at a reception at Vice President Mondale's home in Washington. We had been invited to witness the signing of the peace treaty between Israel and Egypt.

On one of our Temple trips to Israel, March 1973.

In Israel again at the Rabbi Max A. Shapiro Forest, 1976.

AT OUR CENTENNIAL DINNER . . .

University of Minnesota President C. Peter McGrath, his wife, and Susan Bonoff.

Marvin Borman and
Mayor Al Hofstede.

Rabbi Stephan Barack and Governor Rudy Perpich.

Bishop Robert Anderson, Rabbi Barack, Archbishop John Roach, and Rabbi Leigh Lerner.

With Stanley Schweitzer, Temple President during our Centennial year and Marvin Borman, chairperson of the dinner.

The participants at the Service commemorating the Temple's 100th anniversary. Standing: Rabbi Barack, Elliot Kaplan, Stanley Schweitzer, Donald Graceman, Burton Joseph. Sitting: Winky Herman, Ambassador Dimitz, and Marjorie Graceman.

John Derus, chairman of the Hennepin County Board of Commissioners, presents me with a resolution congratulating Temple on its centennial.

With Marian Bearman at our Centennial Service. Marian was confirmed in 1914 and is our oldest living confirmand.

Israel Ambassador Simcha Dinitz (right), U.S. Ambassador to The Netherlands Mrs. Burton (Geri) Joseph, and Burton Joseph, a past president of the Temple and then the National President of the Anti-Defamation League, were all at our Centennial Service in May, 1978. Ambassador Dinitz was our speaker.

CAMP TEKO

The Board of Trustees of Temple Israel
cordially invite you to join
in honoring

Rabbi Max A. Shapiro

for his twenty five years of service
to Temple Israel, Jewish life
and the community.

Friday, June 13, 1980
8:15 P.M. at Temple Israel
An Oneg Shabbat will follow services.

With Senators Boschwitz and Durenberger, and my brother Rabbi Robert at the dinner celebrating my 25th anniversary at Temple.

The participants and committee for my 25th anniversary celebration. Back row: Rabbi Barack, Ardene Meshbesher, Sidney Cohen, Lois Rose, Rabbi Zemel, Elliot Kaplan. Front row: Rev. Witheridge, Arthur Naftalin, Marvin Borman, and Burton Joseph.

RABBI MAX A. SHAPIRO EDUCATION BUILDING

Elliot Kaplan, President of the Congregation, presents me with the mezuzah to be placed at the entrance of the Rabbi Max A. Shapiro Education Building in commemoration of my 25th anniversary.

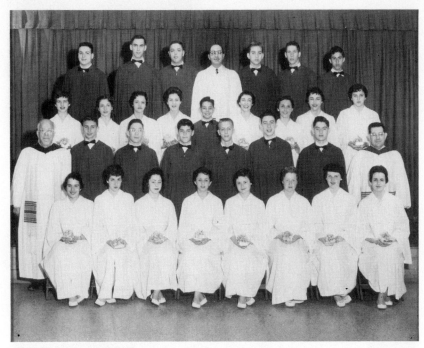

My first confirmation class in 1956 . . .

and my most recent in 1980.